The
American
University

Frank H. T. Rhodes

THE
AMERICAN
UNIVERSITY

National Treasure or Endangered Species?

Ronald G. Ehrenberg

Editor

CORNELL UNIVERSITY PRESS

ITHACA AND LONDON

First published 1997 by Cornell University Press.

International Standard Book Number 0-8014-3350-9

Printed in the United States of America.
Design and composition by Rohani Design, Edmonds, Washington

Librarians: A CIP catalog record for this book is available from the
Library of Congress.

Cornell University Press strives to utilize environmentally responsible suppliers
and materials to the fullest extent possible in the publishing of its books. Such
materials include vegetable-based, low-VOC inks and acid-free papers that are
also either recycled, totally chlorine-free, or partly composed of nonwood fibers.

Cloth printing 10 9 8 7 6 5 4 3 2 1

CONTENTS

v

FOREWORD

I N THE SPRING OF 1995, when Frank H. T. Rhodes retired as president of Cornell University, the faculty thought long and hard about a gift. They wanted to present him with a gift that symbolized not only Cornell but the whole experience, the whole path, we had trod together for eighteen years. We wanted a symbol of the university, a symbol that could be meaningful to a poet, to a particle physicist, to a psychologist, to a professor with extension responsibilities. Finally, we came up with the right answer—a book.

A book seemed to us the proper symbol for what I call the four pillars of our faith. What greater symbol of the creative arts is there than a copy of *Leaves of Grass*. What greater symbol of research than the famous articles Hans Bethe wrote in 1935 on nuclear physics for the *Review of Modern Physics*, which shaped the thought of a generation of theoretical physicists. What greater symbol for education than a student grappling with a complex idea in a book. And, finally, what better symbol of outreach is there than that wonderful American invention of the nineteenth century, those strings of small libraries that brought culture and learning to the backyards of every American and to people who were not privileged to go to the universities. The books that enriched the lives of Americans are to me a wonderful example of the American dream. And I still thrill to see those little libraries in the small towns of America.

But what book? We had to have a book that had personal meaning to President Rhodes but that also spoke to each of these four pillars of our faith: research, education, outreach, and creativity. We had to have a book that symbolized one of the great ideas that has shaped the history of intellectual thought. Certainly, we decided, if you write down the ten best research outputs of the past two hundred years, the work of Charles Darwin must appear on the list.

What about education? We wanted something that every educated man or woman knows about. Darwin's theory of evolution has become an integral part of education and it is hard to imagine a person who could call himself or herself educated without understanding evolution.

What about outreach? If one were asked to choose the book of Darwin's that had the greatest impact on the history of thought, one would naturally choose *Origin of the Species*. But if one sought the book that had the greatest impact on the lives of individuals, it would probably not be that one; for people are not necessarily intrigued with where turtles came from. But indeed, it is hard to imagine a book that has had a greater impact on how people feel about their origins and how their world is constructed than *The Descent of Man*.

I then thought for a little bit about the last pillar, the creative pillar. I could have reached into my pocket and said, "Here is a CD ROM of *The Descent of Man*," but that would not have seemed right. There is something about a book, something that the monks who wrote the *Book of Kells* understood: that the combination of the beautifully illuminated manuscript and the thoughts that went into it is a combination that enhanced the meaning of both. Those of us who have ever held in our hand a beautiful book, who have turned the pages and smelled the leather, know that this is an experience that transcends, amplifies, the experience of the written words.

The gift the Cornell faculty chose was a first issue of the first edition of Charles Darwin's *The Descent of Man.* It gave me enormous pleasure to present that gift to Frank Rhodes upon his retirement, and it gives me equal pleasure to honor him with the publication of this book, a collection of the essays by the illustrious speakers who participated in the symposium to mark his retirement.

PETER C. STEIN
Professor of Physics and Dean of the
University Faculty Cornell University

The
American
University

The American University:
Dilemmas and Directions

Ronald G. Ehrenberg

AS WE APPROACH the beginning of the twenty-first century, America's research universities are among the jewels of our higher educational system. By far the vast majority of Nobel Prize winners were educated or teach at them, and their excellence attracts graduate students from around the world. Indeed, in 1993, temporary residents earned about 25 percent of all the doctoral degrees granted by American universities. In key scientific and engineering fields, the percentages were much higher. For example, that year, temporary residents received 49 percent of the doctorates in engineering and 43 percent in the mathematical and computer sciences.[1] One noted economist/academic administrator has even asserted that of the best universities in the world, two-thirds to three-quarters are in the United States. He added that similar claims of achievement could be made for very few other sectors of our economy.[2]

---

[1] National Science Foundation, CASPAR Database System, vers. 4.5, Oct. 1995.
[2] Henry Rosovsky, *The University: An Owner's Manual* (New York: Norton, 1990), chap. 2.

American research universities clearly are national treasures. Over the past decade, however, these institutions have increasingly come under attack for a wide variety of alleged sins. Further, their economic bases are increasingly being eroded because of budget problems at federal and state levels, coupled with increased demand for resources to meet competing social needs, such as health care. Thus, although American universities are national treasures, many fear they are entering a period of decline and may well prove to be an endangered species.

Why are research universities being attacked, and why are their supporters in both the private and public sectors increasingly less willing to fund them? In brief, the attacks stem from distress over the increases in tuition, which persistently have exceeded the growth of family incomes; the perception that universities are bloated bureaucracies that have overcharged the government for research; the feeling that universities display a lack of concern about undergraduate education and allow their curricula to be dictated by faculty interests rather than by what students should be learning; charges that they are too "politically correct" or not "politically correct" enough; claims that their faculty and student bodies are too diverse or not diverse enough; concerns that university faculty are producing unneeded Ph.D.s (because no jobs exist for their students) in programs that last artificially long so as to facilitate faculty members' research and the teaching of specialized courses; and concerns that some elite private research institutions have colluded with their private liberal arts college counterparts to limit financial aid awards to undergraduate students. Facing attacks of this magnitude and variety, which institutions wouldn't feel threatened.

Each of the authors of the next seven essays addresses one or more of the reasons universities are being attacked. In what follows I briefly summarize some of the key issues each author raises and offer some observations on why America's research universities have gotten to this point and the major challenges they will face in the future. A concluding essay by Frank H. T. Rhodes, president emeritus of Cornell University, whom this volume honors, provides his assessment of the issues and the changes universities must make if they are to remain flexible and responsive to society's needs in the years ahead.

KEY POINTS RAISED BY THE CONTRIBUTORS

William Bowen's essay focuses on the role of American research universities as vehicles of social mobility. Not only have the economic returns to education remained at historically high levels, but over the last decade attendance at institutions of above-average quality has led to higher returns.[3] As one might expect, this has led to fierce competition for undergraduate admission to the leading research universities, and, as a result, the students who are admitted to them have substantially higher test scores than they did in earlier years.

Bowen argues that need-based financial aid policies, which permit students of all income levels to attend leading institutions, are therefore very important. So, too, he compellingly argues, are efforts to provide opportunities for underrepresented minority students to attend these institutions. He believes that these policies, which often fall under the rubric of "affirmative action" or "diversity" policies, are important not only because a sense of "fairness" requires them but also because a diversified student body provides two types of "externalities" for students at the university and for

---

[3] See Ronald G. Ehrenberg and Robert S. Smith, *Modern Labor Economics*, 6th ed. (Reading: Addison-Wesley, 1997), chap. 14, for evidence on the rates of return to college education. For recent evidence on the return to institutional quality, see Dominic J. Brewer and Ronald G. Ehrenberg, "Does It Pay to Attend an Elite Private College? Evidence from the Senior High School Class of 1980," in *Research in Labor Economics*, ed. Sol Polachek, vol. 14 (Greenwich, Conn.: JAI Press, 1995).

society more generally. First, not only do the underrepresented minority students benefit, but so too do the white students, who are exposed to students from different backgrounds and with different perspectives from their own. Second, the society benefits as a whole because these institutions are training future leaders from many groups and backgrounds and, for our society to thrive, members of all groups must have the opportunity to share in its leadership.[4]

Bowen makes three points in response to the well-publicized fact that the test scores of underrepresented minority students admitted to selective institutions are often much lower than those of admitted white students. First, test scores are heavily influenced by a student's parents' income and educational background and, to the extent that minority applicants come from poorer and more poorly educated families, their test scores should be weighted with this fact in mind.

Second, although the average test scores of undergraduate students from minority groups are lower than those of white students, they are about the same as the test scores of white students who attended these institutions forty years ago. Thus, to the extent that the white alumni of these institutions were qualified to attend the institutions forty years ago, so the minority students are qualified to attend today.

Third, and finally, studies conducted by the Mellon Foundation using historical data from several selective universities suggest

---

[4] In recent years, a federal appeals court decision in the *Hopwood* Case that dealt with the University of Texas Law School, as well as a vote by the University of California Board of Regents and a public referendum in California, have barred the use of race in admission decisions in public colleges in California, Texas, and several other states. However, the presidents of 62 leading research universities that belong to the Association of American Universities have reaffirmed the importance of campus diversity and the use of race in admission decisions. See "62 College Presidents Run Ad Backing Use of Race in Admissions," *Chronicle of Higher Education*, May 1997, A32.

that test scores are very poor predictors of academic performance for underrepresented minority students. Indeed, black students with test scores roughly comparable to those of their white classmates tended to achieve no higher grades or graduation rates than their black classmates whose test scores were substantially lower than those of most of their white counterparts.

Claude Steele is among those who have discussed the reasons talented black students do not do as well in college as their test scores suggest they should. He attributes this failure at least in part to the fact that many faculty have low expectations for these students, which the students then internalize for themselves. The students also must live with the pressure that if they fail, critics of diversity policies will use their failure to condemn these policies. Thus, they carry a burden no white students carry.[5]

This phenomenon implies that diversity policies are not working as well on many campuses as they should. So, too, do the reports from many campuses that their student bodies often segment by racial group so that there is little contact between members of the various groups. To the extent that this occurs, some of the externalities that Bowen has hoped for are clearly not occurring.

These findings suggest to me that in the years ahead universities must devote considerably more effort to truly integrating their student bodies by breaking down racial and ethnic barriers on campus, rather than continuing to measure their success at diversifying their student bodies by focusing on the shares of underrepresented minority group members in their total student populations. This will not be an easy task. Given the extent to which American youth reside and are educated in racially segregated communities, our campuses reflect attitudes and experiences that will be hard to overcome.

---

[5] See, for example, Claude M. Steele, "Race and the Schooling of Black Americans," *Atlantic*, April 1992, 68–78.

The title of Charles Vest's contribution, "Research Universities: Overextended, Underfocused; Overstressed, Underfunded," summarizes the dilemma faced by American research universities. Vest begins by explaining how since the 1980s the research partnerships between government and academia have been breaking down. He bemoans the erroneous categorization by policy makers of research as either basic or applied, their failure to recognize research funding as a investment, and their failure to realize the implications for graduate and undergraduate education of cutbacks in research funding.

How should research universities respond in this new, less supportive environment? Vest suggests four specific goals. First, they should operate with increased efficiency and reduce the cost of education. Second, they should improve the environment for learning on campus. Third, they should use information technologies in creative ways to enhance teaching and learning. Fourth, and finally, they should realign graduate programs with the needs of society. All of these goals arise from the realization that the decline in funding has led research universities to readdress their fundamental objectives, as well as seek to improve their efficiency.

More generally, Vest notes that universities must show their supporters that they are capable of change. They must rebuild the public trust, through their words and deeds. They must reinvigorate a commitment to excellence in our society and rekindle excitement about science. Finally, they must build public support for the life of the mind. Vest believes that only if they achieve all of these aims will they gain allies and the financial support they need.

Harold Shapiro and Marye Anne Fox discuss undergraduate and graduate education respectively. Shapiro addresses only in passing the synergy between research and teaching, which many would argue is central to the American research university. Rather, his focus is on the undergraduate curriculum and the claims made by many critics that the curriculum and indeed undergraduate education in general no longer represent what they once did.

Shapiro provides an overview of how the undergraduate curriculum has evolved over time. His underlying message is that a wide gulf has always existed between the educational ideals espoused by critics and what teachers and students actually experienced. Put another way, he rejects the notion that there ever was a "golden age" of higher education in the United States and that we could gain anything by trying to reinstitute the curriculum of that hypothetical period.

Contemporary critics often point to the post–World War II period as the golden age. Shapiro emphasizes that our educational system at that time had many more warts than we care to remember. For example, it ignored the educational needs of the disadvantaged, paid lip service to the myth of shared values, and ignored key differences that have emerged as sources of major tension today. Indeed, charges made today of curricular incoherence, excessive specialization, and failure to project a uniform set of values were heard then as well.

Shapiro acknowledges that undergraduate education is always in need of improvement. Although he believes it is better now than it ever was, he also thinks it appears to have problems because it is not improving as rapidly as society's needs are increasing and because faculty do not devote as much time to improving the curriculum as they do to conducting research. Moreover, faculty may place too heavy an emphasis on discipline-based instruction, to the detriment of a truly successful undergraduate program. Finally, because many political, social, and cultural conflicts taking place in society are being projected on to university campuses, our undergraduate programs often fail to project a set of common values that we should be instilling in our students.

The increasing size, complexity, interdependencies, and differentiation that characterize modern higher education, together with the rapid expansion of knowledge bases and access to higher education, have implications that, as Shapiro emphasizes, are difficult to overestimate. At the same time, curriculum changes rarely represent the triumph of evil over good (or vice versa), although critics may claim they do. Rather, they represent an attempt to meet a new set of responsibilities implicitly placed on universities by society. Shapiro believes that in our current environment undergraduate education should place more emphasis on moral behavior and an understanding of the role of ethics.

What are the chief obstacles to improving undergraduate education? First and foremost, Shapiro believes that it is that we in academia lose sight of the fact that improving education should be our goal and resort to cultural wars rather than rational discourse over issues such as the role of individuals in their communities, the tension between tradition and change, and the reality of differences between individuals and groups.

Marye Anne Fox addresses graduate education. The poor job market in many academic fields in the early 1990s, coupled with declining levels of federal support for graduate students, has led to a lengthening of the times to degree and an increased incidence of underemployment among new doctorates.[6] Faculty in many fields are now engaged in debate over whether the decline in the demand for new doctorates was a cyclical phenomenon or whether it reflected a more long-term shift in the demand for both new doctorates and faculty.

Fox comes down squarely on the side of those arguing for the need for fundamental restructuring of doctoral programs. Given the declining percentage of new doctorates who are likely to find employment in academia, or who will even end up in research

---

[6] See Ronald G. Ehrenberg, "The Flow of New Doctorates," *Journal of Economic Literature* 30 (June 1992): 830–75.

careers, she argues for broadening, rather than deepening, doctoral programs. In her view, these programs should place an increased emphasis on verbal, written, and computational skills, while providing training in a portfolio of disciplines. Someone thinking of embarking on a career as a science journalist, for example, might couple strong technical training with a study of literature.

One might question, of course, whether such training-oriented programs could ever compete successfully with more traditional doctoral programs. Such efforts could fail because they ignore the need, at least in fields of science and engineering, for doctoral students to serve as research assistants. To the extent that faculty first train students and then reap their investment in the students, by employing them over multiple years, any attempt to alter the depth of doctoral programs will have a negative impact on faculty productivity.

I believe that, rather than a modification of the nature of Ph.D. programs, a diminution in their size is more likely. Faculty are already making increased use of "postdoctoral" appointments in their research programs.[7] Rather than establishing broader academic doctoral programs, the trend may well be toward growth in income-earning professional master's programs. Some of the revenue earned from these programs could then be used to support faculty research activities.

The final three essays in the volume—by Hanna Gray, Neal Lane, and Urie Bronfenbrenner—deal with the prospects in the years ahead for specific disciplinary areas—the humanities, science and technology, and social sciences, respectively. Gray does not take the pessimistic view that some commentators have that new directions in the humanities, including critical theory, gender studies, and multicultural approaches, necessarily reflect

[7] See Charles T. Clotfelter et al., *Economic Challenges in Higher Education* (Chicago: University of Chicago Press, 1991), 168–69.

the deteriorating of the discipline and the prospects for genuine scholarship.[8] Rather, she points out that the humanities always seem to be in crisis. This, she asserts, is probably their natural state given that they deal with complex issues that are rarely susceptible to clear-cut solutions and come under persistent attacks concerning their role in society.

As the universe that encompasses the humanities becomes more crowded and complex, it becomes more difficult to define what they are. This may not even be an important question, however, for, as Gray states, "Whether the humanities be conceived as a form of knowing, as a set of disciplines, of methodologies, or of scholarly and educational purposes, or as a way of thinking about and seeing the world, its achievements and possibilities, its questions and dilemmas, any assessment of the prospects for the role of humanistic scholarship and the breadth of liberal education in our universities must come to terms with the implications contained in these issues."

So what does the future hold for the humanities? In part, it depends on the future of universities and humanists themselves. Will they continue to be tolerant of diverse views and diverse understandings about difficult questions? Will they set standards of quality and not tolerate simplistic interpretations? According to Gray, if the answers to both these questions are yes, the future of the humanities is bright. But whether the answer will be yes is an open question in her mind.

The future of science and technology is the topic of Neal Lane's essay. Given the budget realities in Washington, Lane acknowledges that the federal investment in science and technology is at risk and that university scientists will need to do more with less. He argues that to maintain our science enterprise,

---

[8] For a more critical view of the humanities today, see Dinesh D'Souza, *Illiberal Education* (New York: Free Press, 1991).

academic scientists must connect with society at large, educate society about the importance of science in everyday life, and ensure that future scientists reflect the demographic distribution of the population from which they are drawn.

Lane argues that, to win support from government and industry, universities will need to continue to break down disciplinary barriers and focus on developing cross-cutting structures to attack societal problems. In addition, university researchers will need to make more direct connections with scientists and engineers in industry. Finally, he emphasizes the continual importance of closely tying sponsored research to undergraduate education. Government sponsors, he believes, will be more willing to support research if it contributes to the educational mission and the renewal of our scientific and technical personnel.

Urie Bronfenbrenner's contribution emphasizes the fundamental role the social sciences should play in improving our nation's well-being. He argues that the great threats to our nation's quality of life often lie in the social sphere. To give one illustration of his concerns, he points out that the widening income inequality that has occurred in our society has led to a decline in the well-being of the poor in real terms in recent years. The increasing fraction of children growing up in poverty has in turn led to increases in educational failure, high rates of pregnancy among teenagers, and an increased incidence of criminal activities among our youth.

Bronfenbrenner bemoans that although social scientists appear to be as good as scientists at diagnosing problems, they do not appear to be as good at finding "cures." He attributes this discrepancy to the imprecision of social science theory and empirical evidence. Thus, he believes that a major role of social scientists in universities should be to keep students—the leaders of tomorrow—informed about social problems. If social scientists cannot solve the problems, at least they can keep students aware of them.

Bronfenbrenner's pessimism about social scientists' abilities to prescribe cures may well be unfounded. Indeed, as an economist who has devoted much of his career to evaluating the effects of social programs and legislation, I would argue that it *is* unfounded.[9] The social problems we observe often persist because of the unwillingness of the political process to bear the cost of curing social ills, not because social scientists have failed to prescribe appropriate cures.

FACING THE FUTURE: AN ECONOMIST'S PERSPECTIVE

Will America's great research universities make the hard choices that will be necessary if they are to prosper in the years ahead? The authors of the essays in this volume spell out many of the issues facing universities; however, they do not, in my view, always emphasize sufficiently the inherent conflicts that erupt when there is a shrinking resource base. Economists are accustomed to thinking about how institutions seek to maximize objective functions subject to constraints. I will use such a framework in this concluding section to highlight how America's great research universities have reached their current situation and some of the trade-offs they now face.[10]

Each of our major research universities seeks to be of the very highest quality. Each competes for productive researchers who create new knowledge, bring research funding to the university, and help to enhance the university's stature. Over time, as the competition for faculty has heated up, it has led to lower teaching loads. In the words of two scholars, an "academic ratchet" has taken place in which faculty members' expectations about the

[9] See Ehrenberg and Smith, *Modern Labor Economics*, for a summary of how a variety of labor market programs effect the economic well-being of individuals.

[10] David Garvin, in *The Economics of University Behavior* (New York: Academic Press, 1980), was the first to apply such a framework to university behavior.

fraction of their time that should be devoted to research have increased while their expectations about the fraction that should be devoted to teaching have decreased.[11]

Research universities also compete for undergraduate students. They have invested heavily in new academic and nonacademic facilities to attract the highest-quality students because high-quality students enhance the attractiveness of a university to faculty and to potential recruiters of the institution's graduates. The latter, in turn, further increases the attractiveness of the best universities to the highest-quality students, and students flock to these universities because of the "leg up" that the institutions give them in their quest for postcollege employment and educational opportunities.[12]

The quest for outstanding students was facilitated in the past by the low-tuition policies of flagship public research universities and by the major private research universities agreeing in the early 1970s to engage in needs-blind admission policies and, with federal support, to help meet the financial needs of all students who were accepted. As a result of these policies, there has been a great increase in the socioeconomic and racial and ethnic diversity of the students who attend major private research universities, as well as a dramatic increase in the quality of the students, at least as measured by test scores.[13]

Great universities also compete for outstanding doctoral students. These students are important to faculty because of the roles

[11] William F. Massy and Robert Zemsky, "Faculty Discretionary Time: Departments and the Academic Ratchet," *Journal of Higher Education* 65 (Jan. 1994): 1–22.

[12] See Philip J. Cook and Robert H. Frank, "The Growing Concentration of Top Students in Elite Schools," in *Studies of Supply and Demand in Higher Education*, ed. Charles Clotfelter and Michael Rothschild (Chicago: University of Chicago Press, 1993), 121–40.

[13] See Ronald G. Ehrenberg and Susan H. Murphy, "What Price Diversity? The Death of Need-Based Financial Aid at Selective Private Colleges and Universities," *Challenge* 25 (July 1993): 64–73.

they play in research and because their presence permits faculty to teach more specialized graduate courses and fewer undergraduate courses. Teaching needs in the latter areas are often met at least in part by graduate students in their roles as teaching assistants.

In their quest for excellence, great universities are constantly adding faculty in new, emerging disciplines and creating interdisciplinary programs to address social and scientific problems. They are reluctant, however, to eliminate existing programs or fields of study. Indeed, the faculty tenure system limits the flexibility of a university to change the composition of its faculty across disciplinary boundaries.

Tuition increases considerably outpaced inflation at both public and private research universities during the 1980s and in the first half of the 1990s as institutions sought to continue to enhance their quality in the face of stagnating federal and state support. Because real income growth in the economy has been zero or small for many years, tuition increases that outpaced inflation invariably led institutional financial aid budgets to increase at even more rapid rates. As a result, a substantial share of the tuition revenue at many institutions has been plowed back into institutional financial aid, thus diminishing the resources the institution has available to meet other needs. Public perceptions of university costs being "out of control" and of university decision makers being insensitive to the economic conditions facing the families of potential students now limit the ability of private research universities to continue to raise tuition by more than the rate of inflation.

The pressure on the major research universities has increased still further as federal and state funding for higher education has become more limited. Faced with competing social needs and a desire to reduce the size of government, federal and state governments reduced their rates of growth of spending for higher education, and in some cases in the mid-1990s, these rates of growth turned negative. Rather than thinking of federal financial aid programs for undergraduate students and federal funding of university research as investments in our nation's future, policy makers instead began to see large programs that could be cut to help reduce budget deficits.

Thus, our major research universities are truly faced with resource constraints that are increasingly becoming tighter. While one can argue, as Charles Vest does, that they must become more efficient and do more with less, one can push this line of reasoning only so far. Ultimately, these institutions must make hard choices.

Put another way, our research universities will prosper in the years ahead only if they "grow by substitution." Resources to support new and emerging fields will be found only if institutions cut back on some of their activities. Institutions, save for the very richest, will have to be selective in what they seek to accomplish. More and more of them will have to emulate the rare institutions that have publicly cut back on programs.[14]

With diminished support, invariably either university research will be funded increasingly from undergraduate students' tuition revenue or research productivity will decline. There are limits, noted above, on the ability of universities to raise undergraduate tuition, so the latter scenario is more likely. A corollary, however, and a point made by several of the contributors to this volume, is that faculty will need to focus more on their revenue-generating customers and devote more time to undergraduate education. Will faculty understand that the "ratchet" must be reversible and that they must diminish the time they allocate to research? Since a large fraction of doctoral students are funded by

[14] One institution that has boldly done so is the University of Rochester. See Christopher Shea, "At University of Rochester, Bad Times Prompt Bold Measures," *Chronicle of Higher Education*, Dec. 15, 1995, A33–A34.

external research grants, the reduction in external funding for research will also most likely lead to a contraction in the sizes of doctoral programs. These changes will not occur because university administrators value research and doctoral education any less than they did in the past. Rather, they will occur because resource constraints dictate them.

More generally, with diminished resources, universities will have to reexamine many of their policies. William Bowen's essay very persuasively presents the case for needs-blind admission policies, need-based financial aid policies, and aggressive policies to diversify student bodies. I fully agree with his arguments. The costs of these policies may be prohibitive for many institutions, however, and we are already seeing a gradual erosion of them at all but a few institutions.[15]

Universities will also increasingly need to realize that there is a trade-off between the resources they devote to buildings and those they devote to people. Although many major research universities have substantial maintenance needs, spending on both research facilities and facilities designed to attract students (e.g., athletic facilities) is likely to slow down as institutions seek to provide funding to maintain faculty size and start new academic programs.

The abolition of mandatory retirement for faculty, effective in 1994, will also affect research universities. Prior research suggests that the abolition of mandatory retirement will not affect most of American higher education but that it will lead to some faculty at major private research universities delaying retirement until after the age of seventy.[16] This in turn will slow down the flow of new

[15] Ehrenberg and Murphy, "What Price Diversity?"

[16] See, for example, Albert Rees and Sharon Smith, *Faculty Retirement in the Arts and Sciences* (Princeton, N.J.: Princeton University Press, 1991), and P. Brett Hammond and Harriet P. Morgan, eds., *Ending Mandatory Retirement for Tenured Faculty: The Consequences for Higher Education* (Washington, D.C.: National Academy Press, 1991).

doctorates into faculty positions and increase the cost of faculty to universities. The latter will occur because, on average, full professors are paid 60 percent more than assistant professors.[17] These changes will require research universities to think about ways to reduce faculty costs and maintain their flows of new faculty. Options include providing incentives for senior faculty to retire and/or placing tighter limits on the proportions of tenured faculty.

Finally, research universities will have to think more carefully about what new information technologies mean to them. On the one hand, there is the concern that new technologies may reduce the demand for residential undergraduate experiences and thus a major source of revenue for universities.[18] On the other hand, as Charles Vest points out in his essay, there is the understanding that new information technologies can considerably enhance educational experiences. With this understanding, however, comes the realization that in most cases information technology increases, rather than reduces, costs.[19] Furthermore, information technology is a recurring expense, not a one-time investment. Hence, methods must be found to carve funding for it out of university budgets. Whether the result is fewer faculty, less financial aid, or fewer new facilities will differ across institutions, but inevitably such choices will need to be made.

[17] See "The Annual Report of the Economic Status of the Profession," published annually in the March-April or May-June issue of *Academe*.

[18] See Eli Noam, "Electronics and the Dim Future of the University," *Science*, Oct. 13, 1995, 247–49.

[19] An innovative attempt to use technology simultaneously to increase educational quality and to reduce university costs by providing back issues of academic journals on line, thereby reducing library space needs and handling and maintenance costs, is described in William S. Bowen, "JSTOR and the Economics of Scholarly Communication," paper presented at the conference of the Council on Library Resources, Washington, D.C., Sept. 18, 1995.

CHAPTER 1

No Limits

William G. Bowen

AT ITS CORE, the American university is very much the same institution that it has been for some time. In no way is it "endangered." Indeed, the American university is a national treasure, created and developed with ingenuity and devotion and vested with the capacity to serve society into the indefinite future, as it has done since its establishment, in roughly its modern form, in the latter half of the nineteenth century. The American university of today—the "new" American university—is a national treasure precisely because it is, in many respects, the "old" American university.

Is there another institution that embodies as many positive possibilities? I don't think so. Do universities—and those who inhabit them—display an occasional wart? Of course. But their deficiencies, limitations, and occasional absurdities (including self-inflicted wounds) are nothing compared with their positive accomplishments and their potential.

These institutions do not need anything approaching radical surgery. Rather, they need "loving critics," to use John Gardner's memorable phrase: fewer brickbats and more constructive criticism, coupled with words of reassurance and tangible assistance. In particular, they need to be encouraged to retain the virtues that have defined their character. I worry more about the risks of careless transformation, designed to cure a perceived ill of the moment or to respond to a trendy demand, than I do about inertia and rigidities, although I, too, would like to see more flexibility and willingness to adapt in timely ways to new circumstances. In short, I am an avowed believer in the ancient mission of universities: to be centers of learning, where students and faculty learn from their predecessors while simultaneously testing new ideas; to be places where no orthodoxy holds sway, where freedom to dissent is respected as well as protected, where individuals are valued for who they are and what they can become; and, finally, to be institutions that serve as powerful engines of opportunity and social mobility.

Market Tests: Returns and Enrollment Patterns

As a sometime economist, I naturally look to markets for evidence that others value universities as I do. One of the most striking empirical findings of recent years is the dramatic increase in the wage premium associated with graduation from college, as compared with graduation from high school. Between 1979 and 1986, the earnings differential expanded from 32 percent to a record level of roughly 70 percent.[1] Census data for more recent years indicate that this high premium has been sustained—and may even have increased somewhat. There is no great mystery as to what has been happening. The main explanation is that there

[1] Kevin Murphy and Finis Welch, "Wage Premiums for College Graduates: Recent Growth and Possible Explanations," *Educational Researcher*, May 1989, 17–26.

have been shifts in demand for different kinds of labor: our economy is assigning more and more value to higher education as preparation for success in the workplace.

There is also recent evidence that, after controlling at least roughly for ability, economic returns to investments in education are enhanced by attendance at institutions of above-average quality.[2] Certainly applicants appear to be convinced of the value of attending the strongest institutions. At the leading research universities, in particular, competition for admission has intensified, and student qualifications have risen appreciably.[3]

The conclusion is clear: by the most mundane marketlike tests, in which undergraduate students vote with their feet and employers vote with their payrolls, the leading research universities are doing better than ever. (A similar claim can be made at graduate and professional levels, as can be seen by examining the flows of talented students from all over the world into American graduate programs.) It is at least mildly ironic that many of the most vociferous critics of universities are the same people who are most impressed by market tests and are especially interested, I suspect, in enrolling their own children in prestigious institutions.

[2] Sarah E. Turner, "Changes in Returns to College Quality" (Department of Economics, University of Michigan, 1995, unpublished article).

[3] The average SAT scores (verbal and math scores combined) of students at Research I universities are higher than those of students at any other category of educational institution; and between 1973 and 1992, the edge in SAT scores at Research I universities increased. The Research I universities gained vis-à-vis both the Research II universities and the Liberal Arts I colleges. For the Research I universities for which comparable data exist, the average combined verbal and math SAT score rose by thirty-two points between 1973 and 1992. For the Research II universities, the comparable score fell thirteen points (to 1,055); for the Liberal Arts I colleges, the average score fell fifteen points. Whereas the Research I and Liberal Arts I categories of schools had nearly identical scores in 1973 (1,138 and 1,133), in 1992 there was more than a fifty-point gap between them (1,170 versus 1,118). Data were collected by the Andrew W. Mellon Foundation staff, especially Joan Gilbert, Elizabeth Duffy, and Idana Goldberg.

In citing data on economic returns, I do not mean to suggest that the desire to attend the most highly regarded research universities (or the strongest liberal arts colleges) is driven in some narrow sense by a preoccupation with earnings projections. Many other motivations—and other kinds of rewards—are highly relevant. For example, an excellent education increases dramatically a student's range of career options by making possible access to a broad array of vocations, including some that, although not high paying (teaching and social work, for example), are attractive in other respects. Moreover, many of the most remunerative occupations convey significant psychic benefits, which may be as highly valued as the dollar rewards captured by studies of economic returns. Many lawyers and doctors—and even CEOs—enjoy what they do.

In addition, and every bit as important, higher education provides many students with the basis for enjoying a much more satisfying life outside the workplace than otherwise would be possible. Such benefits may include intellectual stimulation—the pure pleasure of learning; greatly enhanced access to the worlds of literature, art, and science; preparation for highly rewarding involvement in civic and community activities; the development of values and personal qualities, including quiet self-confidence; and, finally, the opportunity to get to know other highly talented people, who may become lifelong friends. All of these noneconomic outcomes add immeasurably to the overall return to higher education, and they should not be underweighted simply because they are harder to assess in monetary terms.

Social Mobility and "Pluralism" in America

Research universities serve the public in countless other ways. High on any list of their contributions would be the provision of advanced training, including doctoral education of the highest quality, and the nurturing of scholarship and research in an array of pure and applied fields. For my own part, I identify strongly with the values attached to the pursuit of learning for its own sake, with the civilizing influences that result, and with the lasting qualities of heart and mind that are developed almost unknowingly as byproducts of growing up in highly disciplined educational institutions of the first rank.

Woodrow Wilson, who believed so strongly in the ideal of service, also understood how values—or "character"—are developed in a university, as he made clear in a talk given to the class of 1909 at Princeton:

> I hear a great deal about character being the object of education. I take leave to believe that a man who cultivates his character consciously will cultivate nothing except what will make him intolerable to his fellow men. If your object in life is to make a fine fellow of yourself, you will not succeed, and you will not be acceptable to really fine fellows. Character, gentlemen, is a by-product. It comes, whether you will or not, as a consequence of a life devoted to the nearest duty; and the place in which character would be cultivated, if it be a place of study, is a place where study is the object and character is the result.[4]

There is another way in which research universities, in company with the rest of the country's system of higher education, serve the public. Research institutions remain critically important as engines of mobility—as pathways upward for those from every background who see education as the way to satisfy aspirations that in many cases would have been unimaginable to their parents.

Innumerable studies demonstrate that education has played a critical role—really *the* critical role—in determining occupational

[4] Princeton University archives.

status. To a remarkable extent, education liberates people from their social origins; we know that as access to education increases, the significance of "inheritance" decreases.[5] One of my colleagues, Harriet Zuckerman, summarized the idea this way: "The Horatio Alger myth may still have a grain of truth in it, but the poor hard-working boy who saves the drowning daughter of the town's richest man stands to benefit much more if he is educated than if he is not."

We have heard much lately about the widening distribution of income in America—about the growing gap between the rich and the poor—and its causes and implications. My own conviction is that many people are prepared to accept hard lives for themselves if they genuinely believe their children will have better chances than they themselves had.

I will never forget a conversation with a black mother on the night before a Princeton commencement at which her son was graduating as the recipient of every honor the university could bestow. She had received no schooling beyond the seventh grade and had worked tirelessly her entire life. She was surrounded that evening by family who had come from many places, and in looking at all those people, she said, "You know, Mr. Bowen, my son thinks we are making too much of all this. But you must understand that I knew from an early age that there was a limit on what I could achieve because of my race and my education. I was determined that for my children there would be *no limits*." Surely, promoting the ideal of opportunity for people of all races is both right in principle and essential for the future of our country.

[5] For a compilation of references to the role of education in promoting occupational mobility, see Ernest T. Pascarella and Patrick I. Terenzini, *How College Affects Students* (San Francisco: Jossey-Bass, 1992), especially 426–30. The seminal work on this subject is Peter Blau and O. D. Duncan's *The American Occupational Structure* (New York: Free Press, 1967). The next twenty-five years of research is examined in a series of fifteen papers in *Contemporary Sociology* 21 (Sept. 1992): 596–668.

The most obvious conclusion to be drawn from this line of argument is that student aid deserves a very high priority. Of course, there is room for improvement in how student aid programs are designed and managed at both institutional and government levels. From the standpoint of public policy, we have to be concerned that the political currents of the day could endanger hard-won gains in broadening both choice and access for students from all but the wealthiest families. Only at our peril will we allow higher education to be resegregated along economic lines—or along racial lines, which is at least as great a danger.

DIVERSITY, RACE, AND AFFIRMATIVE ACTION

No cluster of topics in higher education is more likely to offend these days than diversity, race, and affirmative action. When Gary Trudeau of *Doonesbury* fame spoke at Yale University in 1991, he began: "Parents, Friends, Graduating Seniors, Secret Service Agents, Class Agents, People of Class, People of Color, Colorful People, People of Height, the Vertically Constrained, . . . the Eurocentrics, the Afrocentrics, Afrocentrics with Eurorail Passes, . . . the Divesturists, the Deconstructionists, the Home Constructionists, . . . and, God save us, the Permanently Housed at Home. In the spirit of the new plurality," he continued, "I thought I'd begin today by trying to offend all of you at once, in lieu of my usual practice of offending small, informal groups as I go along. If I have left anyone out, I naturally apologize for my insensitivity."[6]

As Trudeau reminds us, in his inimitable way, diversity can be thought of along many dimensions. Furthermore, by focusing on race, and more specifically on opportunities for African Americans in higher education, I do not intend to imply any lack of urgency about issues related to gender or to opportunities for a

[6] Trudeau at Yale University Class Day, May 26, 1991.

wide range of other groups, including whites from Appalachia, immigrants from Southeast Asia and Central America, and so many others who face barriers that may seem impenetrable—and may be impenetrable. Nonetheless, the reality is that much of the recent debate focuses on race-specific issues. The present-day "divides" and tensions are all too evident, as is the history of the black population in America. Echoing W.E.B. Du Bois, the distinguished historian John Hope Franklin has argued eloquently that "the problem of the twenty-first century will be the problem of the color line. . . . By any standard of measurement or evaluation, the problem has not been solved in the twentieth century and thus becomes a part of the legacy and burden of the next century."[7]

It is a mistake to allow the issue of opportunities for black Americans to be framed solely, or perhaps even mainly, in terms of individual rights and narrow notions of "fairness." Fairness itself is a complex idea, and it should not command our attention only at the gates to college. Access to the admissions office, after all, depends on a host of preconditions, and not all groups are treated "fairly." One thinks immediately of differences between public schooling in parts of New York City and public (and private) schooling in many suburbs, not to mention other aspects of inner-city life.

While acknowledging that fairness is a very important objective, especially in a society that espouses individual initiative and the promise of opportunity, we dare not lose sight of the functions selective colleges and universities are supposed to serve in society and of the presence of what the economist calls "externalities." A college or university is in the fortunate position of being able to exercise selectivity in its admissions. At the same time, an institution that has more well-qualified applicants than it can possibly

[7] John Hope Franklin, *The Color Line: Legacy for the Twenty-First Century* (Columbia: University of Missouri Press, 1993), 5.

accept has a far more demanding responsibility than simply deciding which applicants have the strongest credentials as traditionally defined.[8]

To be sure, academic credentials are of primary importance. No one should be admitted, for any reason, who cannot take full advantage of the opportunities a particular institution offers. Thus, it makes sense to start out by limiting the pool of serious candidates to those whose credentials exceed a high threshold. It also makes sense to admit without question the absolutely most outstanding candidates—those at the most rarefied end of the range of whatever distributions of achievement and promise one thinks will best predict future performance. Having discharged those obligations, institutions will be left, almost inevitably, with a group of candidates, often a large group, well qualified for admission, whose credentials are clearly above the threshold but not at the very top.

No individual applicant has the "right," or anything approaching an entitlement, to a place in the class. Each individual deserves to be treated fairly, to be spared irrelevant or irrational prejudices, including inappropriate forms of favoritism, and to be judged appropriately on the basis of known criteria consistent with the mission of the institution. But those charged with making admissions decisions have to be concerned with three sets of considerations that transcend measures such as SAT scores and class rank.

The first set of considerations concerns the predictive power of the usual "objective" criteria. SAT scores and other quantifiable measures tell only part of the story. Any admissions staff with courage will accept the need to include avowedly subjective

[8] My basic views on admissions policies were formed some time ago and are explained in considerable detail in an article I wrote at the time of the Bakke controversy. See William G. Bowen, "Admissions and the Relevance of Race," *Princeton Alumni Weekly*, Sept. 26, 1977, 7–13; reprinted in *Ever the Teacher* (Princeton, N.J.: Princeton University Press, 1988), 422–36.

elements in their assessment of candidates. What is the person's character? How many barriers, including racial discrimination and economic disadvantage, have been overcome? What is the likelihood that the individual will grow significantly in this educational environment and contribute to it? Does the candidate seem to be getting stronger or to have peaked already in achievement?

The other two sets of considerations concern the long-term effectiveness of the institution itself and the obligation of the admissions staff to be alert to the needs of the institution, as well as sensitive to the particular circumstances of specific applicants.[9]

Composition of the Student Body

It is widely understood that the quality of education depends on the full range of students involved in the enterprise. Therefore, any educational institution has to ask whether including a diversity of qualified individuals, with diversity defined along many dimensions, including race, is likely to improve the educational program. Most of those who have taught would respond in the affirmative to this question, for they have taught courses in which another perspective contributed substantially to the discussion.

A personal example, a nonclassroom one, grows out of the intense debate over investment policies concerning South Africa

[9] Kenneth B. Clark, in an interview in the *New York Times* (May 7, 1995), was repeatedly asked how he would handle an admissions case in which "the choices were down to two university applicants of equal qualifications, one black and one white. Whom would you take?" After much discussion and a repetition of the question, Clark responded, "I think I'd take the black . . . *because I think that would help the university*" (emphasis added). Thus, Clark acknowledged explicitly that the university has its own needs and an obligation to meet them. The issue is not just what is best for individuals; indeed, ironically, it may not even be best for a particular black (or white) student to be admitted. Clark is wise to remind us that, in any case, it is legitimate for admissions officers to serve the larger needs of the university and the purposes it is chartered to serve.

that occurred at Princeton and on many other campuses. As painful as the debate was at times, it seemed obvious even to me, a president under siege by black students who thought I was hopelessly conservative on this issue, that the campus community benefited enormously from the presence of black students who cared passionately about race and racism. The campus benefited as well from the presence of enough black students to permit a range of perspectives within that group. A great deal of real education occurred—for everyone. Obviously, there are many other less contentious situations in which simply living with people who are different from oneself breaks down stereotypes and provides new insights into life and the variety of people who inhabit this world.[10]

Can such benefits be readily measured? Probably not, though I am convinced we should try harder to gain a more objective sense of the educational value of diversity. In any case, we have evidence of the "revealed preference" variety. Applicants them-

[10] The presence of a diverse student body of course creates challenges that are far from simple to address. As Neil Rudenstine, president of Harvard University, reminded his audience at a Harvard commencement address on June 4, 1992: "Our species—viewed from a broad historical perspective—has generally been tribal and sectarian; quite passionately attached to political, religious, or other convictions, sometimes with violent results; deeply intolerant of groups or castes or races that have been categorized as impure or inferior or apostate; and highly nationalistic in our modern era—even pathologically so throughout much of our twentieth century."

Thus, it is hardly surprising that we find tensions on every college campus that is making any real effort to accommodate a diverse student body. Why should anyone expect students to throw off, instantly and automatically, the personal and historical "trappings" that they bring with them to college? Why should we expect them to set aside, simply because they now live in a dormitory, the deeply rooted inclinations to be, in Rudenstine's words, "tribal and sectarian"?

Moreover, I agree with Gerhard Casper, president of Stanford University, who said recently, "I think we do not make enough of the fact that, relatively speaking, American universities may be the most diverse and integrated institutions in the world. In spite of various incidents that are played up in the press . . . there are few, if any, institutions that are, comparatively speaking, more successful than universities at encouraging their members to cross bridges" ("Come the Millennium, Where the University?" speech given at the annual meeting of the American Educational Research Association, April 18, 1995, San Francisco).

selves certainly are aware of the value of diversity and would undoubtedly not apply to the leading colleges and universities if their student populations were more one-dimensional. Stated more abstractly, enrolling a diverse class has potentially large educational benefits for many if not all students—and these benefits are widely appreciated. In this sense, as in others, admission is not, as some would have us think, a zero-sum game. Student A benefits because student B was admitted.

Potential Contributions to Society

A college or university, and its admissions staff, must also consider the longer-term benefits to the society at large that come from educating talented students from many races and backgrounds. A principal job of these institutions is to build human capital, for the long-term benefit of society at large. Surely any university that wishes to claim a capacity to train leaders for this evolving world will want to educate students who come from many groups and backgrounds. Does anyone dispute the desirability of having a larger cadre of well-prepared black leaders in business, law, academia, politics, and every other walk of life? We need the talents, as well as the perspectives, of such people.

Moreover, with fewer barriers between cultures, our world is becoming less provincial and our sense of community more pluralistic in its racial and ethnic composition. Without the ability to think outside parochially defined sets of viewpoints, it will become harder for anyone, white or black, to function effectively. From this perspective, there is much to be said for allowing students to gain the experience while they are in college of living, learning, and working with others who are very different from themselves.

Consideration of these societal benefits reveals how the admissions process, thoughtfully managed, can make contributions that go beyond the particular individuals being educated. There are external benefits to be enjoyed by the society at large if we succeed in educating a broader range of leaders, as well as educating individuals from "mainstream" backgrounds so that they will be better able to understand and cope with diversity.

Eventually, this new perspective on diversity should accrue to the hypothetical white student who was rejected even though he or she had a higher SAT score than a minority student who was accepted. Although it is far too much to expect such a student and his or her family to understand or accept this rationale, at least right away, it is just such a long-term view that we should expect American universities to have.[11] They cannot escape the obligation to make hard decisions that transcend the immediate interests of particular individuals. If the admissions/learning process in fact contributes to building a more civilized world, everyone will benefit, including the hypothetical rejected white student and his or her children. Admission to selective colleges and universities is *not* a zero-sum game.

HAS DIVERSITY MADE ANY DIFFERENCE?

Moving from these rather abstract, if critically important, propositions to some empirical realities, it is fair to ask, as many do, whether efforts to increase diversity have made any difference. Are we better off now than we were prior to the advent of affirmative action?[12] There are no rigorous answers to this question

---

[11] There is a considerable literature demonstrating the power of what psychologists call "loss aversion." The point is simply that perceived losses are weighted more heavily than potential gains. For a very insightful application of this line of thought to the debate over affirmative action, see Fredrick E. Vars, "Attitudes toward Affirmative Action: Paradox or Paradigm?" (senior thesis, Princeton University, May 1995).

[12] I tend to avoid the phrase "affirmative action" because of all the baggage it has collected and because it denotes an extraordinarily wide range of initiatives many of us who believe in diversity may or may not support.

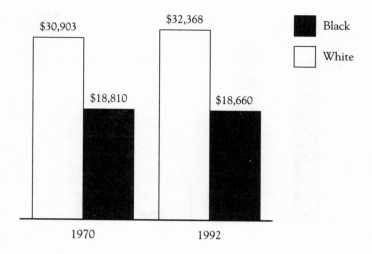

Figure 1.1 Median Income of U.S. Households, 1970 and 1992 (1992 dollars)

because, as always, many moving parts have been moving at the same time. It would be a mistake to assign the full credit (or the full blame) to affirmative action for changes that no doubt are the product of a large set of societal forces. Nonetheless, there are relevant pieces of evidence.

In an attempt to answer this question, some people focus on white-black income inequalities, although these data have to be interpreted with great care. If we examine median incomes of households (fig. 1.1), we find that black households actually lost ground to white households between 1970 and 1992 (the median for black households was 61 percent of the median for white households in 1970 and 58 percent in 1992). This decline is surely due mainly to the increased returns to education over this period, combined with the fact that the absolute level of educational attainment of the black population remained below that of the white population. The median for black households would almost certainly have declined even more than it did, relative to the

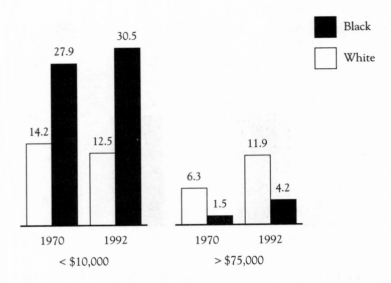

Figure 1.2 Percentage of Households with Income Less Than $10,000 and Greater Than $75,000, 1970 and 1992 (1992 dollars)

median for white households, were it not for the disproportionate gains in educational attainment by blacks over these decades.

Another way of making the same point is that although the fraction of the black population in the lowest income category (below $10,000 in 1992 dollars) increased significantly between 1970 and 1992—from 27.9 percent to 30.5 percent (fig. 1.2)—the share of the black population in the highest income category ($75,000 and up) also rose—from 1.5 percent of all black households in 1970 to 4.2 percent in 1992. This welcome news seems a small intimation of the upward mobility made possible with improved access to the leading colleges and universities.

There is no doubt whatsoever that, both absolutely and relative to whites, there have been marked improvements in recent decades in the educational attainment of blacks twenty-five years of age and older. The gains are dramatic, for both men and women. In 1960, only 18 percent of black males and 22 percent

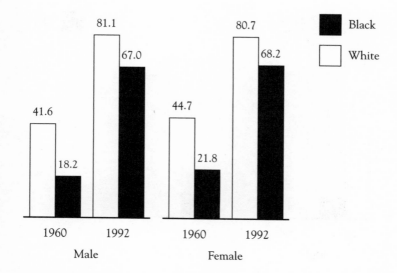

Figure 1.3 Percentage of Population Completing Four Years of High School or More, 1960 and 1992

of black females had graduated from high school; by 1992, however, roughly two-thirds of black men and women were high school graduates (fig. 1.3).

The differential in high school graduation rates between blacks and whites also narrowed significantly. In 1960, the likelihood of a black man or woman graduating from high school was less than half the likelihood of a white man or woman graduating from high school. By 1992, the high school attainment rates for black men and women were, respectively, 83 and 85 percent of the corresponding rates for whites.

Similar progress has been made at the college level (fig. 1.4). In 1960, only about 3 percent of black men and women were college graduates. In 1992, roughly 12 percent of the black population over twenty-five years of age had completed college. Of course, whites continue to complete college in larger numbers than blacks, but this differential has also narrowed considerably, especially for

Figure 1.4 Percentage of Population Completing Four Years of College or More, 1960 and 1992

black men. Whereas black men were one-fourth as likely as white men to have graduated from college in 1960, by 1992 their college graduation rate was nearly half the rate for white men. The gap is still large, but nothing like what it was in 1960.

Even at the doctoral level, where change is always slowest (in part because it takes so long for most students to earn doctorates), there is evidence of at least modest progress (table 1.1). Between 1988 and 1993, the number of doctorates awarded to African American students in the humanities increased from 88 to 112; in the natural sciences, from 89 to 133 (with most of this increase in the life sciences); and in engineering, from 31 to 80.

From the standpoint of the academically selective colleges, trends in SAT scores may be of special interest. Comparisons are possible only since 1976 (fig. 1.5). Over the following eighteen years, the differential in mean SAT scores between black and white test takers has narrowed markedly: by twenty-eight points

Table 1.1 Doctoral Degrees Earned by Blacks, 1988 and 1993

Subject Area	1988	1993
Humanities	88	112
Social Sciences	95	90
Psychology	100	119
Natural Sciences		
Chemistry	21	31
Biological Sciences	48	74
Other	20	28
Sub-total	89	133
Engineering	31	80

Source: National Research Council, Survey of Earned Doctorates, "Summary Report 1988," table 1A, and "Summary Report 1993," table A2.

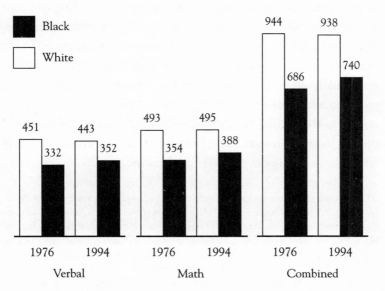

Figure 1.5 Mean SAT Scores, Nationwide, 1976 and 1994

in the case of the SAT verbal scores and by thirty-two points in the case of the SAT math test. Here, too, the remaining gaps are large, and the absolute scores for most black students remain low, at least from the perspective of the most selective colleges and universities. Overall, there were perhaps six thousand black test takers with combined verbal and math SATs over 1100 in 1994, compared with at least 150,000 among whites.[13] Nonetheless, as shown in table 1.1, progress has definitely been made. The greater opportunities for black students to go to college, and to compete for places in the most selective colleges and universities, have without question affected the aspirations and the achievements of high school students.

A study being conducted by the Mellon Foundation is addressing a number of aspects of admissions, in-school performance, and subsequent "life outcomes" using a sample of matriculants in the classes of 1955, 1980, and 1993 at between twenty and thirty academically selective public and private colleges and universities. The study is in its early stages, but pooling the data for what we call the ZED subset of universities provides some preliminary figures based on the experiences of three quite different universities. (To respect promises of confidentiality, the group continually alters the pool of institutions and varies the letters used to identify subsets of institutions.) At this stage, there is no reason to think that the choice of the ZED subsample has biased results, but more information, from more schools, could obviously affect these highly provisional conclusions.

---

[13] The data on means are taken directly from *College Bound Seniors: 1994 Profile of SAT and Achievement Test Takers* (Princeton, N.J.: College Entrance Examination Board), iii. Estimates of the total numbers of candidates with combined SAT scores of more than 1,100 are our estimates, based on percentiles by race and ethnicity provided by the College Entrance Examination Board. We realize that it is incorrect to combine SAT verbal and math scores without knowing the interrelationship between the two sets of scores. For rough estimates, however, this seemed to be a reasonable expedient.

For the university for which the most complete data currently exist, the average SAT score for black matriculants increased substantially between the fall of 1976, when the class of 1980 matriculated, and the fall of 1989, when the class of 1993 started out. The combined verbal and math SAT score for the black matriculants increased about one hundred points, to a level of more than 1200 (roughly the eighty-fifth percentile of the national distribution that includes white students only). At the two institutions for which we have the most reliable historical data, the average SATs for the black students in the class of 1993 are within a few points—six to thirty—of the average SATs for the white students in the class of 1955. Thus, it seems that the absolute standard for the black students at these institutions today is quite high. (Members of the class of 1955 would certainly so testify!)

At the same time, the SAT scores of the black matriculants, while high on an absolute scale, are about 10 percent lower than the average for the white matriculants; thus, the rigorous application of a pure "color-blind" standard, based solely on SAT scores, would have dramatically reduced the numbers of black students enrolled in these institutions. To quantify this proposition: if one imposed the probabilities of a white student being accepted, based on SAT scores, on the black applicants, almost three-quarters of the black students who matriculated in 1989 would have been rejected.[14] These institutions would have been left with about 2 percent black students in each entering class rather than about 8 percent. It seems self-evident that basing admissions on SAT scores alone would have markedly reduced the benefits of having a multiracial student population, for the black student body and for the student body overall.

[14] This formulation abstracts from the many other factors that almost everyone agrees are relevant to admissions decisions by assuming, in effect, that these factors are distributed across the range of SAT scores in essentially the same way for white and black students.

We are at too early a stage in assessing the in-school performance of the black students to present anything purporting to be findings, but we can report two early impressions. First, the black students at the ZED universities appear to have done well academically by almost any conventional standard (graduation rates, grades, honors). Second, and this is perhaps more surprising, initial inspection of the data suggests that the retrospectively "rejected" black students did approximately as well as the "retained" black students. Unlike their white classmates, there is no statistically significant correlation, at least for these black matriculants, between SAT scores and grade point averages (GPAs).

The implication is apparent: applying the rigorous "color-blind" test of identical SAT probabilities and rejecting all those black matriculants who did not fit within the probability structure for whites would have done next to nothing to improve the overall academic performance of the black students, since the "rejected" students did as well as the "retained" black matriculants. Eventually, we hope to learn much more about both in-school performance and how students with various admissions and in-school profiles have fared following graduation; to learn about subsequent educational and occupational histories, incomes, civic and avocational activities, life satisfactions, and so on—in short, to learn about the entire gamut of outcomes, nonmonetary as well as monetary. Any other approach to testing is partial at best, and we would be well advised to postpone serious judgments until the data needed to permit more appropriate tests are available.

Policy Recommendations

Meanwhile, it is clearly worth pondering the meaning of the apparently much looser correlation between SAT scores and GPAs for black students compared with white students (indeed, in the ZED subsample, the absence of any statistically significant correlation at all for the black matriculants). Stanford psychologist Claude Steele has discussed in a most stimulating way the tendency among many highly talented black students to do less well in college than one would have predicted, given their SAT scores. He has suggested that the academic performance of these students has been impaired by the corrosive effects of low expectations and by the stigma associated with "remediation":

> One cannot ignore the distinctive fate of 1980s blacks: a remedial orientation put their abilities under suspicion, deflected their ambitions, distanced them from their successes, and painted them with their failures. Black students on today's campuses may experience far less overt prejudice than their 1950s counterparts but, ironically, may be more racially vulnerable. . . . In criticizing remediation I am not opposing affirmative action recruitment in the schools. The success of this policy, like that of school integration before it, depends, I believe, on the tactics of implementation. Where students are valued and challenged, they generally succeed.[15]

If Steele is right, there are important policy implications. Suffice it to say that the results of efforts to increase diversity on our campuses may greatly depend on what kinds of learning environments are created. One of my colleagues has observed that Steele's analysis inspires admiration for the ample successes achieved by minority students in the face of the forces to which he alludes—but can we find ways to do better in encouraging black students to achieve their full potential? Steele thinks the answer to that question is a resounding "yes," and so do I.

[15] Claude M. Steele, "Race and the Schooling of Black Americans," *Atlantic Monthly*, April 1992, 68–76.

It is easy to understand why growing numbers of high-achieving black members of our society seem to have doubts about affirmative action as it has sometimes been practiced and, more particularly, to be enraged when their own accomplishments are called into question for no reason other than that they are black. That is insulting, to put it mildly. At the same time, as many have pointed out, affirmative action would hardly seem to be the leading cause of the stigmatizing of a black population that has experienced centuries of discrimination, within a society in which ingrained low expectations have created mind-sets that no one should expect to be erased overnight. Nor is it helpful to act as if we have somehow already achieved, or achieved somewhere, at some earlier time, the color-blind society many of us see as the goal. When someone suggested to John Hope Franklin that we return to the ideal of a color-blind society, he responded: "Oh, fine, and when and where did that exist?"[16]

The wiser course of action, surely, is to be realistic about where we are as a society, to take the long view, and to demonstrate both patience and persistence. Beyond that, a few general injunctions concerning admissions apply. First, attempting to substitute formulaic approaches for the exercise of judgment is unwise in the extreme. It robs applicants of their individuality and demeans any selection process.

Second, we should be careful never to confuse the creation of opportunities with assurances of good results. As Mamphela Ramphele, vice chancellor elect of the University of Cape Town, has said, "A student . . . has to take responsibility for his/her academic success or failure. *One cannot . . . claim the right to succeed.*"[17]

[16] John Hope Franklin to members of the Andrew W. Mellon Foundation, March 29, 1995.

[17] Janet Levy, "Interview with Mamphela Ramphele," *Democracy in Action*, Feb. 28, 1995, 5–7, 18 (emphasis added).

Third, we should avoid, to the greatest extent possible, approaches that label students. In the words of a wise friend of mine, we should try to make it possible for everyone to feel "unself-consciously included." One specific issue that needs to be addressed is the support structures available for students (black and white) who need help after they have been welcomed through the door. We must navigate creatively between the most extreme "tough love" approaches and patronizing remediation programs.

Fourth, there are obviously numerous approaches to pedagogy and residential life, as well as to admissions, that can be tried. Institutions should be given—and encouraged to use—considerable flexibility in searching for the best ways of achieving what are, in the end, widely shared goals. Public proscriptions of what is acceptable policy are far less effective than allowing a "thousand flowers to bloom."

Fifth, and finally, colleges and universities should take seriously the obligation to look hard at evidence, based on a careful study of outcomes (both individual and societal), and evaluate their admissions policies and practices rigorously. Because the subjects of diversity and race are so sensitive, there is too often an inclination to rule these subjects off limits—both in campus discussions and in conducting institutional research. That is a tragically mistaken reaction to a difficult set of issues. If we are to learn from our efforts, including our mistakes (however well intentioned many of them may have been), we need to be willing to examine the consequences of specific policies we have adopted, to modify approaches, and to press ahead.

These are genuinely complex issues, for which it is necessary to balance conflicting values and to be willing to make sensible compromises. In talking about the Arab-Israeli conflict, Thomas Friedman of the *New York Times* observed that progress was possible only when people on both sides stopped focusing exclusively on their "rights" (which were thought to be heaven sent and therefore not amenable to discussion) and talked instead about their "interests." Friedman refers to a passage from the Babylonian Talmud that can be translated: "Where there is strict justice, there is no peace. Where there is peace, there is no strict justice."[18]

Many of the most thoughtful people, the anti-ideologues, are often driven to qualified, ambiguous conclusions. If we cannot spare ourselves or others the task of wrestling with conflicting values as well as conflicting ideas, we can at least assure those who accept this aspect of complexity that they are in good company—historically, as well as in the present day. Isaiah Berlin's book of essays, *Russian Thinkers*, is full of examples of the moral dilemmas faced by nineteenth-century Russian writers as many of them sought to balance a yearning for absolutes with the complex visions they simply could not push from their minds. "The middle ground," Berlin wrote, "is a notoriously exposed, dangerous, and ungrateful position."[19] Today, as in nineteenth-century Russia, that is precisely the patch of ground to which we are often driven if we grapple honestly with most problems of the moment.

Where better to find that patch of ground than at a research university? Where else should that patch of ground be so respected and protected?

[18] Translation provided by David Weiss-Halivni, a rabbinical scholar at Columbia University. Friedman referred to this passage in a speech he gave at Princeton University on April 2, 1995, and then in his column in the *New York Times* of April 5, 1995.

[19] Isaiah Berlin, *Russian Thinkers* (New York: Viking Press, 1978), 297.

CHAPTER 2

Research Universities: Overextended, Underfocused; Overstressed, Underfunded

Charles M. Vest

THE DIVERSITY AMONG American universities is one of the great strengths of our system of higher education. But although their styles and missions may vary, our research-intensive universities have all been the beneficiaries of a common legacy: a national policy framework that has supported them since the end of World War II. Indeed, our national science policy gave birth to the most successful system of higher education in the world. In this sense, they share a common history, and together they have conferred upon our country its position as the world leader in science and education.

Today, the framework of that national policy is metastable at best—weakened by a lack of a common vision and trust and by a loss in our national will to excel. Our research universities are overstressed and underfunded, and much of this strain is the direct result of our changing world and changing federal policy.

Fifty years ago, the policy basis for federal support of research and education in America was outlined in a report by Vannevar

Bush, an adviser to Presidents Franklin Delano Roosevelt and Harry S Truman. That report, entitled *Science: The Endless Frontier*, drew on the experience of the scientific community in World War II and provided the vision for national science policy for nearly half a century to come.[1]

Bush argued that it was the government's responsibility to promote "the flow of new scientific knowledge and the development of scientific talent in our youth." Such an investment in research and education was essential, he said, for the promotion of health, prosperity, and national security, and it was in the nation's best interest to "strengthen the centers of basic research, which are primarily the colleges, universities, and research institutes."[2]

Thus was created the underlying social contract that enabled the American research university to define itself, to achieve world preeminence, and to give bright young men and women from all social and economic strata access to the best in higher education. The universities and the federal government shared a common vision and commitment that served the nation and the world very well indeed.

NATIONAL POLICY: NEW DEVELOPMENTS, NEW DANGERS

Since the mid-1980s, when I began my career as a senior university administrator, I have seen that partnership frayed by a steady instability in policies and budgets, rule changes, investigations, institutional harassment, and deepening misunderstanding. The nation, led by the federal government, has steadily added missions and requirements without sustaining the resource base to meet these new and changing requirements. We now have an

[1] Vannevar Bush, *Science: The Endless Frontier* (Washington: U.S. Government Printing Office, 1945).
[2] Bush, 3, 2.

overextended system that discourages many of our best young people from pursuing careers in academic science.

One of the main reasons this is happening has to do with de facto shifts in responsibility for setting science, technology, and education policy. Over the past few years, a great deal of policy making has in effect moved from the executive branch to Congress—a Congress that not only reflects a changing set of social values but that has lost much of its institutional memory.

This is not to say that our universities are without fault. College administrators mistakenly assumed that because universities were unique and important, they never needed to change. These administrators have tended to take for granted the respect and confidence society placed in them and have turned a deaf ear to legitimate concerns.

In this strained environment, our national R&D pendulum has begun to swing fast and wide. These swings are manifestations of the vagaries of a political system in a world of rapid and unprecedented change. They also are indicative of a pell-mell search for policy in a time of fundamental change.

Especially worth noting are three potentially disastrous policy-related errors: (1) the inaccurate, unhelpful, and, in part, partisan categorization of research as basic or applied or strategic; (2) the failure to recognize research funding as an investment; and (3) the separation of the goals of research and education in federal funding of universities.

Beginning with the first of these policy errors, in 1993 a Democratically controlled Congress decreed that large portions of federally supported university research should be strategic in nature, that is, it should have reasonably well-understood relevance to defined national needs, especially those associated with increasing our national competitiveness. Just two years later, many House Republican leaders declared that it was a proper and important function of the federal government to fund "basic" research in universities. In their view, "applied" research had a lower priority, and most "applied" programs did not make the cut as budgets came down.

To be only slightly simplistic, in 1993 the watchword regarding government sponsorship of research was "strategic" or "applied." Today, it is "basic." "Applied" research, according to this new view, should be done by industry; thus, only the market will decide what should be done and universities will not have a role in the "applied" arena.

What is being called "applied" seems to refer more to which federal agency funds the research than to its substance. I refer here specifically to the role of the mission agencies—the Department of Defense (DOD), the National Aeronautics and Space Administration (NASA), and the Department of Energy (DOE)—which currently support more than 70 percent of all federally sponsored research in America's engineering schools and provide more than 70 percent of the federal support for graduate students in these schools. If bias against so-called applied research continues to erode support for the research budgets of these agencies, it will badly weaken fields such as electrical and computer engineering, materials science, and mathematics—the very fields on which a bright economic future depends.

Projects in science and technology and programs in advanced education cannot simply be started and stopped at will. Nor can they undergo major changes in direction every few years. The nation requires a reasonable degree of continuity and long-term perspective if it is to produce the results the nation needs. To do so, we need to rebuild *bipartisan* support and understanding of the goals and mission of the federal government in the sponsorship of university research. If the partisanship presaged by the debates about strategic, basic, and applied research expands, the nation will not be well served. We need to recover and reaffirm a national commitment to excellence in federally funded research and to encourage a rigorous competition for the award of scarce national resources. Arbitrary categorical boundaries will serve only to hamper our pursuit of the very best we have to offer.

The second policy error stems from a failure to recognize that research funding is an investment. Rather, there is an increasing tendency these days to characterize funding for research as a cost. It is not a cost. It is an investment—an investment in the future of our human capital—people and their ideas. It also is an investment in the financial sense of the term. A variety of studies in recent years have indicated that the annual return on investment in research and development is on the order of 25 to 50 percent.[3] Even the General Accounting Office reviewed the modest literature on this topic and concluded that these are reasonable figures.

Michael Dertouzos, director of MIT's Laboratory for Computer Science, has noted that over the past three decades the Department of Defense funded some $5 billion (1995 dollars) in research in information technology. This funding resulted in between a third and a half of the major breakthroughs in information technology—a sector of the economy that today accounts for some $500 billion of this country's gross domestic product. Even if we make the very conservative assumption that the DOD funding resulted in only one-third of today's computer industry, that is a 3,000 percent return on investment.

No matter how imprecisely we may quantify it, investment in research and graduate programs pays substantial dividends and must be viewed as a wise financial investment for the nation. The wisest investment of all, however, is in the education of the next generation. That is more important now than ever.

That brings us to the third policy error—the separation of education and research when it comes to federal funding. The

[3] See, for example, "Supporting Research and Development to Promote Economic Growth: The Federal Government's Role," report prepared by the National Council of Economic Advisors.

most valuable and farsighted concept to emerge from the original Bush vision was that by supporting research in the universities, the government would also be investing in the education of the next generation—a beautiful and efficient concept. In short, every dollar spent would be doing double duty. This integration of teaching and research is at the heart of America's unique system of research universities.

The integration of teaching and research is in danger of disintegrating because the government is paying less and less of the actual cost of the research it sponsors—with the result that tuition and gift revenues, which should be going directly to pay for teaching, are being tapped to make up the difference. In addition, cost-related policies are producing incentives for faculty to employ postdoctoral fellows and professional researchers rather than to support graduate students. This is very unwise, to say the least. The following two statements from the National Institutes of Health (NIH) illustrate my points:

> NIH may be adjusting payments to Research Graduate Assistants so that payments do not exceed rates of pay to postdoctoral appointees at each university. NIH views both RGAs and postdoctoral appointees as salaried positions.

> We believe that the actions of a prudent person would not include providing greater compensation to individuals who are less qualified by education and practical experience than others performing similar work.[4]

This myopic vision regarding research procurement is radically different from the eloquent and sensible vision of Vannevar Bush. We must turn back from such policies. The interweaving of

---

[4] "Graduate Student Compensation," report prepared by the Department of Health and Human Services, Office of Inspector General, Oct. 26, 1994.

education and research is at the very core of our universities and of the federal policy that makes them possible. But policy changes and changes in costing rules are driving out opportunities for students to learn by doing research, at both undergraduate and graduate levels. We must retain the notion that research and education are integrated, mutually reinforcing activities. If we do not, the quality of both will suffer.

CHANGES NEEDED IN OUR RESEARCH UNIVERSITIES

It would be easy to lay all the problems of research universities at the feet of the government and to say that it is the government that needs to change. Our universities also need to change—in a number of ways—if they are to enjoy the confidence of society and do their best in serving society.

I would like to suggest four specific goals to which our universities should aspire. First, our universities need to be operated with increased efficiency and quality, so that faculty and students can be better supported. Universities especially must reduce the cost of education, as felt by students and their parents. Second, we need to improve the environment for learning on our campuses. Third, universities must learn to use information technology in creative new ways to enhance teaching and learning. Fourth, universities need to do a better job of realigning their educational programs with the needs of society, particularly at the graduate level.

Increasing the efficiency and quality in our institutions must, of necessity, be a matter for concerted action during the next few years. These times call for direct attention to the effective and efficient management of the affairs of our institutions.

American industries have learned a great deal about how to add more value, how to improve the quality of what they do and produce, and how to become more cost-effective. In many instances, the improvements have been dramatic. Despite the fundamental differences between industry and academia, the experience and techniques developed in corporate America hold important lessons for those in the academic world. The terminology of reengineering and quality-driven enterprise is harsh to academics' ears, but the methodologies of industry are worth learning; research universities need to adapt and employ these methodologies in their institutions.

Reducing the cost of education will not be easy. As the government pulls back its funding of research and its support of students, universities are pressed to make up the difference. How do they do this? The answer is with gifts and with income from endowments—funds that should be going directly to support teaching programs and at a time when the rate of return on endowments is slowing.

There are indications that the situation, especially regarding federal sources of funding, is about to get much worse. Yet, although fundamental forces are acting in opposition, universities must strive to bring their costs down, to remain affordable and accessible to their students.

Our universities are magnificent institutions that provide historically unparalleled opportunities for students and faculty. There is an exhilaration, a commitment to excellence, a drive, and a rapid rhythm that make our institutions exciting, vital, and effective—especially for our best-prepared and most highly motivated students—but the human touch has eroded.

Along with the excitement and exhilaration comes a pace of activity that is relentless. Faculty are overextended, particularly as they compete for research support in an increasingly difficult climate, while students crave more personal interaction with faculty. Academia, ironically, has become a place where quiet contemplation and sustained deep dialogue are in increasingly short supply.

There is the will to correct the problems, but the efforts to do so run into two mounting obstacles. The first is the need for universities to increase their efficiency and lower their costs. The second is the growing diversity of academic communities, a situation that brings with it still greater need for personalization and for an increasing breadth of social issues and student aspirations to be addressed.

Suggesting that information technology be applied to learning might seem like a counterintuitive response to the problem of how best to provide more personal approaches to teaching. Yet, in my professional lifetime, computing has moved from being an esoteric mechanism for scientific calculation to being a ubiquitous, if somewhat undisciplined, tool for analysis, exploration, and communication. It links us together across time and space in unprecedented ways. Using tools like the World Wide Web, students already have easy, instantaneous access to information and people from all over the world. Information and ideas circumnavigate the globe in the form of text, graphs, photographs, sound, and video images. Group work—even across great distances—is about to be accomplished in radically new ways.

We have just scratched the surface of what these technological advances mean for universities. Over the next decade, there will be many experiments involving new ways of delivering education over long distances. Each of our institutions will have to make explicit decisions about what role it wishes information technology to play in its mission.

The tools of the interactive media are too powerful not to play a profound, positive role in improving learning and education, and undoubtedly their role will be in ways we cannot yet envision. The technology itself will not be a panacea, but it will likely contribute significantly to helping students gain efficiency in learning and to aiding universities in lowering the costs of education. The flexibility of technology may be helpful in addressing the varied needs and paces of learning of increasingly diverse student bodies. It will contribute to the globalization of education, as students and teachers interact and share resources across national boundaries.

There are many who argue that the use of information technology in education will lead to greater dehumanization of the learning environment. Many faculty at MIT, however, are moving toward a different conclusion, which is that the applications of information technology to education may lead to learning becoming *more* personalized. It may be that many professors will take on more of the role of guide, mentor, and tutor, while technology will play an increased role in obtaining, formatting, and presenting information. In this sense, we may be moving back to the future.

This future may seem distant to some, but it is just around the corner. Not only must we be ready for it, we also must shape it. This will require faculty and others in universities to rethink much of what they do, and not only how they teach but what they teach.

There is yet another way in which universities need to prepare for the future—that is, by realigning their educational programs with the needs of society. My concerns have to do particularly with the structure of graduate degree programs. Simply put, universities need to shorten the time it takes to get a graduate degree, to prepare students more solidly for the world of practice, to place greater emphasis on cooperative learning and achievement, to define postgraduate career opportunities in broader terms, and to encourage students to draw on the interactions among a variety of fields and institutions. I am thinking primarily about education in engineering, science, and management, but I suspect these considerations should be extended across the liberal arts and other professional schools as well.

To be more specific, engineering education is entering a period in which increasing emphasis will be placed on preparation for modern industrial practice. The powerful foundations of science, mathematics, and computing that have been constructed during the past four decades will remain, but an increased emphasis on preparation for practice and a somewhat reduced emphasis on preparation for research careers will become the norm. This does not imply a movement to training rather than education. Quite the contrary. It means there will be increased emphasis on synthesis and design, attention to process and production, consideration of social and economic context and complexity, and more emphasis placed on working in multidisciplinary teams. The normal entry point for an engineering career will be the master's degree. There will be somewhat fewer engineers with doctorates.

Graduate education in science seems in less need of modification. At least as a *gedanken* experiment, however, we should consider master's-level science education a respected preparation for entry into industry, government, and other careers. Doctoral students in science also need to be given a broader vision of a scientific career. There is life for scientists beyond academia and beyond the dwindling number of high-powered government and corporate research laboratories. Society would benefit greatly from having scientifically trained minds contributing to a wider variety of professions. This shift in outlook should be accomplished with vision and purpose—not grudgingly.

Management education will change and become more diverse in the decade ahead. The American romance with the traditional MBA program seems to be waning. Corporate expenditures of time and money for now-traditional forms of continuing executive education also are being greatly attenuated. Universities should offer more diverse forms of management education in which more interaction with the real world is included. In particular, genuine interaction *must* be developed between management and engineering schools.

In the future, universities will develop more compact and focused forms of management education, tailored to individual companies or industries, often delivered in part through interactive information technology. Another dominant theme in every school will be the internationalization of management education.

Finally, faculty must be encouraged to engage in truly interdisciplinary research and education, to pursue the wondrous opportunities for advancing knowledge at the interfaces of traditional disciplines. Research must deal with the full scale and complexity of issues like those of the earth's environment and economic sustainability—issues that require efforts that span the social and physical sciences, management, engineering, and the humanities. This is the intellectual frontier, the new opportunity to perform a service to society and to fulfill an obligation to future generations of scholars.

THE REAL CHALLENGES

The following section spells out what I think are the real underlying challenges causing the stresses, overextensions, and funding problems universities face.

First, universities must change. They do not like change, but they must become less fearful, less resistant, and more responsive to it. The post–Cold War era has brought rapid change in this country's economic and political outlook, in our population, and in the opportunities before us. Yet, ironically, our universities— society's premier agents of change—are cautious and extremely slow to change. In part, this is because those of us who are affiliated with universities hold certain values, activities, and attitudes to be of such enduring importance as to be unquestionable. We become defensive and do not question our own operations and thoughts as we exhort others to do. This cannot continue. If we do not get serious about responding to change—and indeed lead it—our value in the eyes of the public and many of our patrons will decline, and this decline may be well deserved. Deserved or not, it will accelerate the decline in financial and moral support for what we do and what we believe in.

We must rebuild the public trust. There still is goodwill and support in our society for colleges and universities. This support, however, is a mile wide and an inch deep. It is fragmented and very vulnerable. The nation's opinion leaders—journalists and politicians—have a much more negative view of universities than does the general population, but those of us affiliated with them still live with the fallout of several years of congressional and press attacks that created a false image of massive financial irresponsibility and scientific misconduct. As Representative George Brown said in 1995 at an MIT gathering: "The savage politics of budget cutting will inevitably lead to cuts in research funding over the next seven to ten years for every field imaginable. . . . The scope and scale of these cuts will depend on your efforts to mobilize your community and educate your legislators and the public on the importance of your work."[5]

It is not only the general public whom educators must educate. We must instill in our graduates a broader and deeper understanding of their own universities. Too frequently, our harshest critics are poorly informed alumni and even former faculty members. This is an indicator of how much work universities have to do to regain the public trust. We need bold and concerted action—through our words and our deeds—to convince our patrons and our students of the wisdom of investing in our institutions and in our collective future.

Universities must reinvigorate a commitment to excellence in our society. This nation has lost its will to excel. Perhaps this is a natural response in a relatively peaceful era in which our economy has been weak, but it creates an atmosphere that has permitted a rise in various forms of populism that do not value institutions and that question anything having the appearance of elitism or privilege. Analyzing or explaining away our predicament does not change the situation, however. America has to stop wallowing in negative journalism and visionless politics.

[5] MIT Club event, May 9, 1995, Washington, D.C.

If we in research universities are to do our best and contribute the most, we must regain a national will to excel—a belief in excellence and a commitment to the future. To foster such a goal, academic leaders need to be teachers and sources of inspiration to a much broader public than we seem to reach. This will require listening to the dreams, aspirations, and values of people in this country. I suspect that far too many people simply do not believe that what happens on our campuses broadly represents the values and views of the nation; in other words, they do not believe those in research universities speak to them. (Nothing has so fed this view as the excesses of debate regarding "political correctness.")

Those in universities must rediscover and articulate a vision of the national interest. Too often, policy makers and opinion leaders hear only the narrow message of institutional and individual self-interest. We must all raise our sights together.

Those in universities must also rekindle excitement about science. For quite understandable reasons, the public and the government are placing greater emphasis on the *payback* of investing in scientific research—payback in the form of improved economies, industries, and quality of life. These are extremely important aims. Still, we must work harder to teach students and the public to appreciate the adventure and joy of seeking fundamental knowledge and objective truth. We should talk about what we do not know as well as about what we do know. We should talk about the great mysteries and challenges. We must explain the significance of discoveries.

Excellence, trust, and excitement about science—and perhaps even responsiveness to change—all ultimately depend on respect for the life of the mind. America has never been noted for its public intellectualism. We have a bent toward the practical, and we value doers over thinkers. But the pendulum has swung too far—we value just about everything and everyone else more than we value thinkers. Far too many people treasure the credentials we bestow more than the substance of the education that takes place on our campuses.

None of the obstacles facing universities will come down until we speak more eloquently and more directly both to our students and to the broad public about the value and joys of the life of the mind. We must take care not to justify academic institutions by utility alone. Science is struggling to regain its public voice. The humanities and the arts must be heard as well. Those at research universities must be teachers—speaking both to the contemporary practical needs of society and to its deepest values and moral issues. And, like all good teachers, we must listen, understand, and empathize. Only then will we gain allies, understanding, and support.

In my own dream for the future, the American research university will be a wellspring of scientific knowledge and of technological innovation. Faculty and students not only will find new ways to analyze the complex and pervasive issues facing the nation and the world, they will contribute profoundly to their solution.

Universities will better reflect in their students, faculty, and staff the changing face of America. They will find ways to instill the excitement and romance of science and mathematics in new generations of young people. They will rekindle our nation's belief in the importance of scientific research and education, and of the life of the mind more generally. They will serve our nation well but also will be of and for the greater world community. Above all, those in the academic world will share with their students the leading edge of human knowledge and invention and their passion for making a difference in the world.

CHAPTER 3

Cognition, Character, and Culture in Undergraduate Education: Rhetoric and Reality

Harold T. Shapiro

L IKE AN ARCHAEOLOGIST, I hope with this essay to remove some of the accumulated debris that has distorted our common memory and hampered our clear perception of the undergraduate curriculum, its history, and its relations to the larger society. The "three Cs" of the title represent three of the principal categories that have often competed for influence in shaping the undergraduate curriculum, raising the question of whether the principal focus of undergraduate education should be on cognition, on the production of a certain character type, or on the promotion and nourishment of certain cultural values and traditions. The subtitle reflects my observation that a wide gulf has always existed between the utopian rhetoric of educators, the biting satire of their critics, and the reality of the classroom experience of faculty and students.

My primary objective is to provide a useful, historical frame of reference for discussions regarding the evolution of higher education in America. This is both an overly ambitious effort—since one cannot hope to do more than provide a partial sketch of the evolution of undergraduate education in America—and a very narrow approach—since it will not do justice to the full range of challenges currently facing higher education, including the much-discussed issue of the critical synergy between teaching and research that is so central to the contemporary American research university. Nevertheless, since teaching undergraduates remains the single most important responsibility of the nation's colleges and universities, even a partial approach to the issues may be helpful.

After considering the relationship of the university to the society that sustains it, I will focus on the characteristics and development of undergraduate curricula in America since colonial times in the hope of shedding some light on current controversies and providing a realistic assessment of past accomplishments and future possibilities. I will then focus more specifically on two important and often overlooked components of undergraduate education—the liberal education tradition and the responsibilities of universities in the area of moral education.

Development of Higher Education in America

The history of higher education spans a long period of time, although just how far back the relevant history goes is open to some dispute. At one extreme it has always been true that some people knew more than others—that is, had a more advanced education—and one can find some evidence of "advanced" training almost throughout the historical record. At the other extreme, some would claim that the contemporary university is so distinct from its forebears that we need look no further back than to mid-nineteenth-century Europe or the post–Civil War era in America.

Although it is clearly true that in many parts of the world scholars and their students have been assembling together for learning, study, and the development of scholarly techniques for well over two millennia, the Western university—as a distinctive social organization—was recognizably established only in medieval times. Needless to say, it incorporated some ideas and institutional arrangements developed elsewhere.

Although the contemporary Western university stands today considerably transformed from its medieval profile, it owes a good deal of its social organization and legal form to rather remarkable institutional innovations introduced in twelfth-century Europe. The twelfth century marked a great revival of learning in the West, and the development of a new social institution, the medieval university, with its privileges and protected status, was part of this revival.

We have clung proudly to this medieval ancestry for many reasons, but chief among them were that these medieval institutions, at their best, represented a far more open and diverse institution of learning than any that preceded them; provided special protection to the student and scholar; developed refreshing ideas regarding the fair assessment of achievement; and formed a kind of international community of learners united by a common language (Latin), a common church (Catholicism), and a common commitment to advanced education. Not only do important aspects of these medieval roots remain alive and well, but the educational ideas that developed at the height of the Greek classical period and the rhetorical schools of ancient Rome also made significant contributions to what we understand today to be undergraduate education.

As a number of scholars have begun to point out, however, our understanding of what faculty actually taught in different eras, what students actually learned, and the meaning of these activities to all participants has often been based on rather superficial sources.[1] Indeed, until recently, historians paid little attention to

---

[1] See, for example, Anthony Grafton and Lisa Jardine, *From Humanism to the*

higher education, since its impact on society before the nineteenth century was considered marginal. Our general knowledge
of these matters is often equivalent to the level of understanding
to be gained regarding the status of the U.S. economy by reading
product advertisements and the speeches of business or union
leaders and/or political figures running for office.

Unfortunately, most of the easily accessible material regarding undergraduate education—in America and elsewhere—can
be characterized as a kind of propaganda in which educators and
other promoters portrayed themselves and their colleges with a
particular variant of utopian oratory. In virtually all cases a huge
chasm existed between articulated educational ideals and actual
classroom experience, as educators through most of recorded history were unable to find the human and/or the physical resources,
or a viable set of institutional vehicles, to fulfill their aspirations.

As in many other areas of our cultural history, purely literary
and/or rhetorical treatments of these issues, as presented in such
works as F. Scott Fitzgerald's *This Side of Paradise* and Upton
Sinclair's *The Goose Step*, often have had more powerful influences on our national imagination than has a careful analysis of
the actual historical record.[2] In any case, for too long, most of us
have been content with unexamined myths that often reflect
nothing more than the wishful thinking of ambitious educators or
the carping satire of their opponents.

Humanities (Cambridge: Harvard University Press, 1986); Gerald Graff, *Professing
Literature: An Intellectual History* (Chicago: University of Chicago Press, 1989);
Lawrence Stone, "Social Control and Intellectual Excellence: Oxbridge and
Edinburgh, 1560–1983," in *Universities, Society and the Future*, ed. Nicholas
Phillipson (Edinburgh: University Press, 1983), 1–29.

[2] F. Scott Fitzgerald, *This Side of Paradise* (New York: Scribner, 1920); Upton
Sinclair, *The Goose Step: A Study of American Education* (New York: Albert and
Charles Boni, 1936). See also George Santayana, "The Genteel Tradition in
American Philosophy," in *Winds of Doctrine* (London: J. M. Dent and Sons, 1913),
186–215, and Thorstein Veblen, *The Higher Learning in America* (New York: Viking
Press, 1935).

Since more recent work by social and intellectual historians is finally providing new and more meaningful insights into the historical and cultural reality of higher education as it has affected students, parents, teachers, and citizens in different eras, it may be time to reconsider certain hallowed clichés about the nature of undergraduate education.[3] Of particular concern is the almost pervasive sense not only that at some previous moment undergraduate education in America experienced a "golden age," in the sense that all constituencies believed the program to fit unusually well with society's expectations, but also that we could gain some considerable benefit now by reinstituting the guiding values and/or the classroom experiences of this bygone era.

Such an era probably never existed, or at least not in those periods when universities played an important social and cultural role; the fact is that until this last century most Americans had little use and/or respect for higher education. Further, disagreements regarding what to teach and how to teach it have been with us for a long time—and contemporary anxieties about such issues as curricular incoherence, excessive specialization, and the failure to project a unified sense of values are, in some important respects, little different than the controversies of yesteryear. Nevertheless, some observers suggest that the best candidate for such a golden age would be the decade or so between the early 1950s and the early 1960s, when higher education was rapidly expanding and the scientific ethos (universalism, disinterestness, empirical verification, and so on) was becoming ever more dominant. At the very least, it seems to many who were educated in that era that this period was indeed one in which there was a general coherence concerning curricular matters, a good balance between the universities'

---

[3] See, for example, Grafton and Jardine, *From Humanism to the Humanities*; Graff, *Professing Literature*; Stone, "Social Control"; Francis Oakley, *Community of Learning* (New York: Oxford University Press, 1992).

commitment to education and research, and wide agreement on the desired nature of the undergraduate experience.

This rosy perception (or misty recollection) may also reflect the afterglow of World War II, when many believed in the wisdom of the existing "American way" in most matters, or it may reflect the excitement that surrounded the growth of both higher education and the increasing dominance of U.S.-based scholarship, or it may simply reflect the self-satisfied autobiographical reflections of educators who grew up during the war. It is true that in the early postwar period, the steady expansion in the quality and quantity of secondary education, together with rapidly increasing public investments in higher education, was creating a new structure of possibilities and making possible the implementation of ideas and hopes that had been germinating for more than half a century.

The postwar years certainly were exciting times in higher education, but also during this era of extraordinary expansion in student access, universities managed to ignore the needs of the educationally disenfranchised, were quite content with the myth of a community of shared values and experiences—that is, ignored questions of differences—and devoted far less attention to what was actually going on in college and university classrooms than to other concerns related to growth and scholarship.

Before examining these points in more detail, it may be helpful to set forth a summary—almost a caricature—of my views of the current situation in the United States.

First, undergraduate education is certainly in need of substantial improvement. Indeed, it is necessary for all faculty to renew and/or expand their efforts in this arena.

Second, although vastly improved over previous eras, undergraduate education has not improved as quickly or responded as successfully to the needs of society as have faculty efforts in research.

Third, although undergraduate education overall has probably never been better, this fact is obscured for at least four reasons. First, being better than ever is not the same as being good enough. Second, the curriculum as currently constituted reflects the disciplinary and scholarly organization of university faculty rather than the independent imperatives of a successful undergraduate program. Thus, the views and discussions of most faculty and "educators" on undergraduate education are more closely tied to their disciplinary commitments and research efforts than to independently conceived undergraduate educational objectives or to the reality of the classroom. Simply put, the fact that disciplinary concerns are so often taken as the key guide to faculty and administrators' aspirations and rhetoric regarding the undergraduate curriculum frequently not only undermines their conversations with those outside the academic community but distorts their own views of alternative possibilities. Furthermore, since many scholarly categories are themselves in some flux, even intraacademic discussions are often confused. That is, faculty and administrators in some disciplines probably need to rethink the basic categories that provide structure to their curricula and make meaningful their understanding.

Third, many of the political, social, and cultural anxieties of our age, such as reconciling individual rights, group interests, and traditional values, have been projected onto the curriculum of our nation's colleges and universities in a manner that has shed more heat than light. As the work of Aristophanes teaches us, this is not a new phenomenon.[4] In this last century, however, the particular anxiety that has shaped much of the controversy over university education programs has been the ongoing struggle between an intellectual vision that is secular and that focuses on the development of both the independent individual and new knowledge and an alternative intellectual vision that is less secular, emphasizes common cultural commitments, and focuses on traditional values.

[4] Aristophanes, "The Clouds," in *Three Comedies by Aristophanes*, trans. William Arrowsmith and Douglass Parker (Ann Arbor: University of Michigan Press, 1969), 16–28, 40–42, 68–81, 102–9.

In the last three decades, this anxiety has been heightened by the new angst of difference, or diversity, which has made it more difficult to blend commitments to both individual and community.

Fourth, universities find themselves at a moment in our national life when the value of all commitments—especially those financed by public funds—is being reexamined and questioned. Within higher education, current criticisms are often received quite out of context and are incorrectly interpreted as attempts to minimize or deny the value of the role of higher education in national life.

Social Purposes/Educational Controversies

In the most general sense, one may think of education as a means—composed of social and curricular arrangements—by which society provides each new generation with many of the capacities, beliefs, and commitments necessary to achieve important societal objectives. Typically, different groups have diverse educational objectives, and as a result many distinct but usually interdependent and often similar educational systems or subsystems exist side by side.

These diverse objectives may cover a wide range and may include the accumulation of certain cognitive and technical abilities as well as an understanding of important cultural values, which in some eras, such as colonial America, were thought of as one and the same. Education may also take place in many venues, including the home, the community, and the workplace, and within formal and specialized institutions. Moreover, even these specialized institutions, as Lawrence Stone has pointed out, often have noneducational objectives as well, such as keeping young adults and/or older children amused and out of harm's way.[5]

---

[5] Stone, "Social Control."

At any historical moment, the particular array of institutions of higher education (and their associated curricula) that society supports reveals a great deal about its views regarding such significant issues as who should receive the most advanced education, the importance of traditional values, the importance attached to innovation and new ways of thinking, the most important sources of knowledge and wisdom, the value placed on particular cognitive abilities, the most highly prized virtues, and the nature of the broad hopes and aspirations of the society itself.

Since these issues are critical to all communities, it is hardly surprising that there has always been considerable controversy regarding the appropriate nature—and curricula—of the formal and specialized institutions of higher education that society sustains. Nor is it astonishing that these controversies are most heated in societies such as ours that have become characterized by rapid change and a very rapidly accumulating knowledge base and that, as a result, specialized institutions of higher education have become increasingly important, indeed almost a requirement of a fully expressed citizenship.

What is absolutely critical is that institutions of higher education, their curricula, and their scholarly and other programs are all designed, or should be designed, to serve some civic purpose. To put the matter simply, teaching and research are a public trust. Even for Cicero, the idea or civic purpose of higher education was to produce cultured and articulate individuals (i.e., orators) who were prepared for active service in civic life.[6] It is the various civic purposes served by colleges and universities that provide the foundation for their social legitimacy.

In a sector as heterogenous as higher education in the contemporary United States, the idea of civic purposes must be

[6] J. E. Siegel, *Rhetoric and Philosophy in Renaissance Humanism* (Princeton, N.J.: Princeton University Press, 1968).

understood as requiring different responses from differently situated institutions; however, these institutions cannot be defended and should not even be imagined as designed to preserve a portfolio of medieval privileges granted to students and scholars and/or to preserve any right of teachers, scholars, and students to special entitlements not enjoyed by other citizens. The special freedoms and privileges enjoyed by university communities are surely mechanisms to enable universities to meet their responsibilities more effectively.

It is helpful in this respect to recall some of the heated debates in nineteenth-century Britain surrounding the effort by some to rouse Oxford and Cambridge from the semimoribund state into which they were perceived to have fallen. One eager participant in the attacks on these ancient centers of learning, Sir William Hamilton, noted that "the University is a trust confided by the state to certain hands for the common interests of the nation."[7] If one accepts such sentiments, and I do, then issues such as university autonomy and traditional academic values, privileges, and responsibilities need constantly to be reexamined in light of the primary civic functions being served by higher education.

Of course, statements such as Hamilton's, even if accepted, do not settle all the important issues, for they still leave those in higher education to decide what is meant by "common interests" or "civic functions," since there are always competing views on such issues. In what way and with what types of educational and scholarly commitment should each university meet its responsibilities? In whose hands should the university be placed? Obviously, the answers to these questions will not and should not be the same for every college and university.

[7] Sir William Hamilton, *Discussions on Philosophy and Literature, Education and University Reform*, 2d ed. (1853; reprint, London: Longman, Brown, Green and Longmans, 1953).

Nevertheless, the concept of civic responsibility helps define the questions that need to be addressed and how, for example, one might think of such issues as the autonomy of universities. Within such a context, the issue of autonomy is not viewed as an ancient right that must be defended but in terms of its current civic function; that is, the focus shifts to clarifying in what way the autonomy of universities serve and promote the underlying civic responsibilities of higher education. There are excellent answers to such a question, but they are seldom articulated. Moreover, in the evolving world environment, these common interests and civic functions often cross national boundaries. Many universities are no longer simply local or national institutions.

Over time, of course, the functions and responsibilities of higher education have changed. Indeed, as the historical record makes clear, no facet of education has proved exempt from the impact of social change. Furthermore, the ongoing accommodation between the various aims of education (old and new) has generated not only a continuing level of controversy but new educational arrangements (curricula and institutions).

Many of the issues underlying these discussions are never fully settled but only temporarily resolved—so that we may take some action—while exploration of new approaches continues. For example, one perennial theme has been the appropriate balance between "liberal," "vocational," and "professional" education. Indeed, this issue arose in ancient Greek discussions and in medieval times and has ever since. Another hardy and continuing issue has been the value of critical and speculative philosophy versus the authority of traditional values. This particular issue is found in ancient Greek sources (e.g., the Sophists vis-à-vis Socrates and Plato), in texts from medieval times, in the wisdom literature from the Old Testament (e.g., the Book of Proverbs versus the books of Job and Ecclesiastes), and in St. Paul's warning to the Colossians to be wary of philosophy and empty deceit.

Fortunately, the continuing curricular tensions created within higher education by such debates have generated many important insights and innovations.

The critical point is that in a changing environment the university will inevitably be drawn into debates about the relationship of its existing programs and commitments to the changing needs of society. Such discussions cannot and should not be avoided. In particular, such dialogue should not be viewed as undermining the traditional values and autonomy universities cling to so strongly. Rather, it is through this dialogue that the most important traditional values, such as autonomy, can be reinforced. Indeed, autonomy, as opposed to slavery, implies a level of responsibility and thoughtful responsiveness that make such a dialogue imperative. Moreover, the history of American higher education reflects, at its very base, the need for continuing examination of the relationship between the polity and the educational institution. Unlike many of the great European universities, the first American colleges were not established by independent groups of faculty and students, or by royal initiative, but by private and public communities to serve important civic purposes. This was one of the first of the distinctively American contributions to the social structure of higher education.

Finally, as American universities look ahead, there is no avoiding the fact that questions of difference, the fact that we do not all share the same values and experiences, will remain central to efforts by our increasingly diverse society to define itself. These differences bring new responsibilities to the university concerning the development of both new ideas, such as how to resolve the tension between the individual and the community in a new context, and curricula. Universities not only need a constantly refreshed vision of their role that reflects the emerging reality of their times but the intellectual energy to enable those in the society to envision universities as an important component of the society's vitality.

HISTORICAL ECOLOGY OF UNDERGRADUATE EDUCATION

In sketching the historical evolution of undergraduate education in America, I will employ a rather broad brush to highlight several points, although I acknowledge that this approach will miss many important variations on these broad themes that certainly need to be brought into the discussion at some stage. Without this more detailed analysis, our understanding will inevitably be incomplete. For example, the curricular story that I will "narrate" does not deal directly with the impact of the tension—eventually resolved—between pagan and Christian understandings of learning, despite the lasting influence of this struggle on Western educational ideology. The particular focus of my "narrative" will be on the nature of the gap between stated curricular objectives and their actual achievement and between our common historical memory and historical reality.

The entire history of higher education will be divided into only four principal curricular periods. This seems to be the minimal number of divisions that enables a coherent story to be told. Briefly, these eras are the classical period (Greek and Roman higher education); the period of scholasticism (the high medieval period); the period of Renaissance humanism (the sixteenth through the eighteenth centuries); and the modern period, which began about a century and a half ago.

The modern period has been characterized by, among other features, the increased size, scope, and responsibility of colleges and universities; the introduction into the undergraduate curriculum of engineering, applied science, science, and preparation for graduate education; the disciplinary organization of curricula; a focus on innovation and critical thinking; and a new idea about the meaning and objectives of a liberal education. The increased size, complexity, heterogeneity, and differentiation that characterize the modern higher education sector, together with the rapid expansion of the knowledge base and access, are changes whose impact is hard to overestimate.

These four principal curricular periods contained a good deal of diversity within them, and the periods themselves often exhibited considerable overlap. Moreover, despite the slowly evolving changes in the nature and objectives of the curriculum, some traditions continued to inform all the periods. For example, the veneration of various classical texts—the list itself being often redefined—for their perceived cultural and moral lessons and/or for the special mental discipline their study required remained an important element, especially before the modern period. This intense, ongoing, and increasingly sophisticated study of revered texts made many contributions to the development of scholarly techniques but always retained within it a potentially conservative streak that, from time to time, caused academic communities to be "stuck in a rut." Nevertheless, our understanding and use of these texts change and evolve in important ways. For example, the new literary sensitivities, or aesthetic appreciation, that Renaissance humanism brought to literary texts not only changed attitudes toward Homer's and Vergil's work, among others, but also added new "classics" to the curriculum.

Two key points are worth recalling concerning the evolution of higher education during these four periods. First, the transformation of the undergraduate curriculum from one era to another was seldom a case of good triumphing over evil or of a more powerful educational ideology replacing a less forceful one. More often, these changes represented the adoption of new undergraduate programs to meet a fresh set of civic responsibilities in a different era. Although both scholarship and pedagogical tools steadily improved, the most important curricular changes were inspired by new societal needs. It is to be expected, therefore, that discarded educational ideologies may one day be reclaimed as suitable once again for a fresh set of circumstances. For example, as Anthony

Grafton and Lisa Jardine have pointed out so effectively, the victory of Renaissance humanism (a literary education committed to
preserving a canon of classics) over medieval scholasticism is perhaps best explained as the victory of a form of education more
amenable to European society in the sixteenth century.[8]

Although the humanists brought into being new scholarly
tools for understanding literary texts and the ability to imagine the
development of modern literature, their approach to undergraduate education was a better fit with the newly emerging European
elite, characterized by its relatively closed governing circles and
distinct lack of enthusiasm for debate on political and social issues.
The elite needed an indelible cultural seal, and the humanist curriculum provided it. It was, as others have observed, a victory of art
and literature over society and polity. By contrast, scholasticism,
with its rigorous training in logic and semantics—complemented
by professional education in medicine, law, and theology—had
been better suited for European society of the fourteenth and fif-
teenth centuries, with its more fluid social elite and its ongoing
struggles for power between the church and the state.

Second, in all of these four principal curricular periods, the
actual experience of students and faculty was dramatically different from the grand plans of educators. Nowhere in the Roman
world could one actually attend a school and get systematic
instruction in the *Septem Artes Liberales*. Nor would we find in the
experiences of students and/or faculty in late seventeenth-century
or eighteenth-century Oxford (when the colonial universities
were being formed) much that was attractive about their actual
academic experiences—whatever the objectives and educational
ideology of the academic program were.

Undergraduate education in America initially grew out of
the Renaissance/humanist curriculum, which had replaced

---

[8] Grafton and Jardine, *From Humanism to the Humanities*.

scholasticism as the framework of undergraduate education in both Britain and continental Europe. As the classical period, with its attention to rhetoric, various components of the *Septem Artes Liberales*, the great literary epics, and a small bit of logic, had given way to the focus of scholasticism on the dialectical and logical analysis of both Christian and pagan texts, so scholasticism itself had given way to the deeper literary tradition of the Renaissance/humanist curriculum. It was this tradition—which placed little emphasis on speculative and critical philosophy, preferred rhetoric over logic, and focused on the aesthetic qualities of the text and a particular sense of virtue, the good citizen, and moral philosophy (i.e., moral control, obedience, and deference to authority)—that the colonists endeavored to transplant to the frontier of Western civilization.

AMERICAN EXPERIENCE: THE COLONIAL AND ANTEBELLUM PERIOD

While the colonists were intent on bringing to America an academic program drawn directly from the Renaissance/humanism/ Reformation tradition, it also is quite possible to claim that undergraduate education in America began as professional education. It seems clear that the colonists had two principal ideas in mind in founding their colleges. They were the preservation of what they believed were the most important aspects of Western learning, including, of greatest importance, Christianity, and the training of citizens to fill key posts in the new society, namely, in the clergy and government service. Moreover, the preservation of Western learning and professional training called, they believed, for much the same educational program—a humanist education focused on the bible and classical literature. It is significant that from the colonial period through the Civil War era, Protestant evangelical movements provided most of the impetus for the expanding higher education sector. Indeed, in the colonial college, little separated the Sunday sermon from the Monday class. What was sought was a kind of intellectual indoctrination in which yesterday's wisdom was passed on to tomorrow's leaders.

The curriculum of the colonial college was designed to sustain an understanding of medieval and Renaissance learning and to create, within the student body, a personal piety and a passing acquaintance with the bible, classical languages and literature, and Renaissance art and literature considered suitable for America's cultural elite, as well as perhaps a little mathematics and natural philosophy. Thus, although the undergraduate college curriculum was designed both to develop the mental faculties of the students and to ingrain in them the habits of "right" thinking (as opposed to innovation and/or criticism), its raison d'être was professional training and the preservation of Western culture. Innovation and critical thinking were the last things on anyone's mind, and pedagogy in the colonial college remained dominated by a rhetorical tradition of rote learning and recitation. The educational theory behind this curriculum assumed that a special moral character inhered in both the linguistic and cultural content of classical languages and literature and that a special mental discipline was imparted by their study—a rather suspect psychological theory.

In the classroom, the reality was grim. Poorly or barely prepared students, coming from an environment with no organized secondary education, encountered—at best—modestly prepared faculty. Few books were available, and, in any case, classroom pedagogy continued to reflect an oral rather than a written tradition: memorization and recitation were the primary pedagogical tools. Thus, while the basic educational philosophy sought to bring Renaissance humanism to bear on uniquely American needs, there is little from this experience we would voluntarily copy and/or wish to apply to our current academic programs.

Even as American higher education approached the Civil War period, there were few well-prepared students and few well-prepared faculty, and the classroom experience was more numbing than exhilarating. The number of colleges had expanded much faster than the number of qualified students, and a good deal of the undergraduate experience centered on essentially remedial work. Even by the end of the nineteenth century almost half of all undergraduates entered higher education through the college's preparatory departments. The eve of the Civil War may have marked the ebb tide of undergraduate education in America. All this is not to say, however, that it did not accomplish the objective of providing a certain cultural "seal of approval" to a small part of America's social elite and its clergy.

POST–CIVIL WAR PERIOD

It is often remarked that a certain vocationalism has always characterized American higher education. Like "PC," however, "vocationalism" is a term usually used by a protagonist to hurl at an opponent. Perhaps it is more accurate to say American higher education—especially at its most formative moments—has been characterized by a sensitive recognition of its civic role. Higher education in America, whether public or private, has always drawn its most creative energy from the desire to meet its civic responsibilities. The transformation of American higher education in the post–Civil War decades provides an excellent example.

In the post–Civil War period, the need for change in higher education became ever more apparent. America was changing, new scholarly disciplines were emerging at a rapid rate, and the world of scholarship and education was being dramatically transformed. A revival and transformation of higher education had begun in Europe (particularly Germany), where new ideas regarding the unity of research and teaching and academic freedom had begun to take hold. This followed a period of growing faith in the primacy of reason and cognition, in the potential and desire for material progress, and in the responsibility of educated individuals to engage in independent and innovative thinking.

In America, this translated into an understanding that the capacity to learn and develop new ideas—to innovate—had become an immensely practical goal. The historically innovative notion arose that society could benefit, economically and in other ways, from institutions of higher education that—for the first time—were centers for free, open, and thoughtful debate (concerning society and science); deliberative and critical practices that were noncoercive; and the development of new knowledge and understanding of all kinds.

The rapid transformation of American higher education in the postbellum period did not occur without considerable controversy, however. While Harvard's president, Charles Eliot, was espousing, in 1869, the benefits of a new "elective" curriculum, Yale's president, Noah Porter, was lamenting, in 1871, the surrender of education to "popular prejudice" and "popular humors." Porter and others were genuinely concerned that the modern subjects afforded no adequate substitute for the traditional curriculum. Despite Santayana's early and biting comments, the "genteel tradition" of the American college and its programs of undergraduate education did not pass quietly into the night.[9]

Nevertheless, as the twentieth century approached, the civic function of higher education in America increasingly was seen as requiring (1) the incorporation of engineering and applied science (basic science was added a little later) and other specialized expertise into university faculties and curricula; (2) the professionalization of faculties; (3) the development of a disciplinary structure for both programs and governance; and (4) the adoption

[9] Santayana, "The Genteel Tradition."

of new organizing principles that focused on the development of new knowledge, graduate education, and a more critical and discerning understanding of the society and its beliefs. As a result, the small paternalistic colonial college with its central focus on the piety and morality of students and its fixed curriculum centered on the study of classical languages and literature gave way, over time, to the larger, more secular university. Thus, in the latter half of the nineteenth century, America began to refashion its institutions of higher education to incorporate important aspects of the research-oriented universities being established in Germany.

Equally important to the evolving profile of American higher education, however, was the distinctively American concept of the land grant university. It was this latter institution that became the chief vehicle for introducing experimental science, a broader spectrum of professional training, and a new level of access to higher education. These developments, together with the fuller development of primary and secondary education and the gradual transfer of authority from the university's trustees and president to the faculty, laid the critical foundations for the full emergence of the American research university half a century later. In the process, the higher education sector became much more heterogeneous, both intellectually and socially. Yet even today the echoes of this transition reverberate—as with, for example, the frequent calls for colleges and universities to focus once again on those traditional spiritual values that could counter the "crass materialism" and "spiritual wasteland" of modernity and offer an antidote to "mere" science and progress and "rampant individualism."

As the modern American university assumed its current form, not only was there a great clash between the advocates of humanism and "professionalism" for cultural leadership of the university and its undergraduate curriculum, but there also a loud clamor about the growing gulf between scholarship and the perceived needs of undergraduates. Concern among many faculty regarding the loss of cultural and disciplinary common ground brought about by growing enrollments, the expanding scope of the university curriculum, and the increasing specialization of the faculty and the freedom of students to select majors was genuine and has remained—for various reasons—an issue until this day. The resultant loss of a sense of solidarity and shared goals within the faculty was regretted by many. Specialized, disciplinary-based scholarship would, it was claimed with some justification, narrow the area of common cultural interest. Concerns about "community" arose as soon as innovation and independent thinking became central to the university's mission.

Irving Babbitt—concerned about the dominance of philology—asked, "Will scholarship dehumanize literary study?"[10] He was hardly alone in opposing some of the new developments.[11] Few remembered that this issue had raised its head much earlier in Germany when Friedrich von Schiller, in his inaugural address at the University of Jena in 1789, made the classic distinction between specialists—who want nothing to distract them—and the "philosophical minds"—who see knowledge as a whole and attempt a more unifying integration.[12] As with many of the important ongoing controversies over the principles and structure of academic communities, this issue has received continuing exploration and reexamination.

Concerns over "community" began to be heard on the nation's campuses just as the nature of a liberal education was being transformed from "indoctrination in right thinking" to the development of quite a different character type. Yet the nostalgic

[10] Irving Babbitt, *Literature and the American College: Essays in Defense of the Humanities* (Boston: Houghton Mifflin, 1908).

[11] See, for example, Theodore J. Ziolkowski, "The Ph.D. Squid," *American Scholar* 59 (Spring 1990): 177.

[12] Quoted (in translation) in Theodore J. Ziolkowski, *German Romanticism and Its Institutions* (Princeton, N.J.: Princeton University Press, 1990), 239.

desire to compel consensus by adherence to some specified set of moral claims, which characterized higher education for so many centuries, continues to mark our contemporary national rhetoric with respect to higher education.

In retrospect, it is sobering to note how little the intellectual needs of the new student body or the emerging needs of the nation figured in some of the nineteenth-century debates—and their successors. The rhetoric certainly failed to reflect the character, challenge, and difficulty of the actual experience of students in the classroom. Quickly forgotten in a collective attack of amnesia were the realities of undergraduate education in the late nineteenth century, such as the following:

- Most undergraduates had ceased to take their undergraduate curriculum seriously and perceived the curriculum, as F. Scott Fitzgerald noted somewhat later, as "an education . . . barren of ideas."[13]
- Most undergraduates found the recitation sections that made up a good deal of the curriculum to be intellectually deadening. In many colleges, the extracurriculum organized by student societies exhibited much more intellectual vitality than the formal curriculum.
- Undergraduates' access to books and/or libraries remained severely restricted.

It sharpens our perspective on these matters to realize that the now much-maligned lecture was received, at the turn of the century, as a breath of fresh air and an important pedagogical innovation.

The overall story of how U.S. higher education was transformed in the period between the Civil War and the eve of World War II is well known, and the full tale will not be repeated here.

[13] Fitzgerald, *This Side of Paradise*.

A few points concerning the nature and quality of undergraduate education during this period are worth noting, however.

First, throughout the early part of this period (1870–1914), the U.S. secondary education system was still in the process of being mobilized. Simultaneously, of course, the formal conceptions of the undergraduate curriculum were being revolutionized. In such "new" disciplines as engineering, science, social science, and, in some cases, the transformed humanities, a curriculum was being created almost de novo. Attempts were also being made to develop a new sense of America in the context of unfolding world events, as well as to preserve some of the more traditional elements of the curriculum. With so much change, it is not surprising that curricular controversies continued as the century began to unfold. Once again, however, the experience in the classroom changed at a much slower rate.

Second, through the 1920s and 1930s, most undergraduates still did not consider their college education a serious intellectual affair. This was the era of "the gentleman's C," college friendships, and "living it up" on campus. Regular class attendance and intensive study were frowned upon. For most students, college life seemed best described as a way to postpone adult responsibilities.

Third, the increase in size, complexity, and heterogeneity of higher education introduced a range of issues, as did the creation and transformation of the disciplines. These conceptual developments were only slowly manifest in the classroom. It took considerable time to build faculty and student bodies both willing and able to take on the challenges of new curricula and pedagogies. Indeed, we have yet to appreciate fully the impact of the increasing heterogeneity of students, faculty, and subject matter on the nature of the civic responsibilities of higher education.

As the basic structure of the contemporary university, with its specialized departments and its commitments to scholarship and graduate and professional programs, was being put in place, however, it was the boom in undergraduate education that directly and/or indirectly provided the financial base on which to build the specialized faculties required for graduate education and scholarship. The impact of these developments on the undergraduate curriculum itself would not be fully realized until decades later.

Although the form and content of the changing programs in universities remain issues for debate, the sheer growth of the higher education sector in the last century is indisputable—and without historical precedent. Older institutions expanded and transformed themselves. New institutions were formed, and a greater variety of postsecondary institutions developed to meet the needs of a changing society and a rapidly expanding student body.

The links between higher education and society became more varied and complex, and the influence of the state on university programs, reflecting both its own increasing investment and the growing importance of higher education, became much more marked. After all, one of the most salient characteristics of higher education in the modern era is that it makes very large demands on other people's resources.

Post–World War II Period

The broad range of new initiatives that transformed American higher education in nature, scope, size, and heterogeneity in the post–World War II decades is also well known. Key developments included the G.I. Bill, major investment in state universities, federal government support of university-based research, expanded student aid policies, the development of community colleges, and the broad expansion of overall access. Among these initiatives, the G.I. Bill was perhaps the most innovative, since it reflected a qualitatively new attitude toward the benefits of higher education.

Throughout history, as long as war has been waged, returning soldiers, if victorious, have received some kind of reward for the service they rendered to the state. In its most primitive form, they were given permission to loot whatever they could and to carry off men and women as slaves. At a slightly more symbolic level, the reward took the form of a land allotment or a payment of currency to the returning soldier. These more traditional rewards, however appropriate or inappropriate, were designed to provide rather immediate gratification, so that military victory and its material rewards were closely related in time.

In 1945–46, however, the United States established an entirely new form of compensation. With the passage of the G.I. Bill, for the first time in the history of the world, society declared that a worthy reward might take the form of an education. One of the startling characteristics of this idea was that not only were the benefits of this prize postponed but the recipients had to do more work before either they or the society could realize the dividends of the investment.

In any case, given the educational infrastructure (ideas and institutions) that was slowly developed and built in the first half of the century, the American university was finally able to take remarkable advantage of the synergies between teaching and scholarship and to improve both its teaching and research programs dramatically. During the postwar period the number of students rose many fold, public policies shifted several times, fields of scholarship were transformed, and America's universities became, for the first time, a critical component of the nation's evolving innovation system. It is only in the last half century that the university and its undergraduate curriculum have demonstrated a continuing capacity for useful experimentation and change.

The emergence of institutions devoted to education in the context of a constantly renewed search for new ideas must be considered a rather radical and distinctive achievement. At its best, the university became a place for dialogue between generations, between cultures, between past and present, and between alternative approaches to understanding. For the most part, it is only the contemporary university that has recognized and incorporated into its curriculum the inevitability of complexity and ambiguity and the need for competitive views in most of the important issues confronting humankind and scholarship. It is able to retain its coherence as an academic community through its shared beliefs in the open pursuit of truth and understanding, in a commonly held set of rational and humane standards to govern the modes of scholarship, and in the ultimate value of the products of the mind.

Given the current pace of change in the national and global environment and the complex mission of higher education today, certain tensions are inevitable. Among them are those between current circumstances and aspirations; the university's role as educator (requiring closeness and responsiveness) and critic (requiring distance and skepticism); specialization and integration; the demands for scholarship, the demands for education, and the demands for other services the university provides; and the increased demands for diversity and for community.

Consequently, the "right" profile in all areas of the university's efforts and programs will remain elusive and controversial. Indeed, the current portfolio of responsibilities of American higher education carries with it the risks inherent in an enterprise that must decide what is to be taught and how it is to be taught and that must also engage as society's "official" critic in the development of new ideas. This is always a risky and uncertain project and continues to require both a closeness and a sensitivity to society's needs and beliefs and an ability to avoid being captivated by society's current beliefs, social values, and priorities.

Despite these tensions, the constant shifting of public policies, the enormous growth in enrollments, the constantly expanding knowledge base, and the ever-expanding portfolio of educational programs, undergraduate education in America has enjoyed decades of rising quality. Yet, for several reasons, this substantial accomplishment has been underrecognized.

First, the broadening scope of educational commitments, together with expanding enrollments, has undermined the university's role as a cultural agent for a small "elite." Second, the need for advanced training in a wide range of fields has perhaps arisen faster than the joint capacities of our secondary and postsecondary institutions to satisfy this need adequately. Third, the United States is experiencing a significant period of transition as it is forced to adapt to a major realignment of world production and to the loss of its dominance in technology and innovation. This transition in the economic and social structure of American life has produced a sense of loss that some observers believe a "proper" university education might repair. Fourth, and finally, universities and their curricula have not yet met the increasingly obvious need to rethink long-held notions regarding both certain scholarly categories and the relationship between individualism and community in a way that will enable scholarship and education to flourish in an environment that is much more conscious of its diversity and the existence of certain irreducible differences. We are faced, therefore, with the paradox that the quality of our accomplishments in undergraduate education goes unnoticed and/or is overwhelmed by other factors that will require painful adjustments in the years ahead.

Two particular aspects of contemporary undergraduate education have received little attention but can have a great influence on the nature of the undergraduate curriculum: the development of new ideas on what is meant by a liberal education and changing attitudes regarding the nature of the university's responsibility in the area of moral education. With respect to the changing notions of a liberal education, I refer to the renewed focus on speculative philosophy, critical methods, and the production of a new character type. On the issue of moral education, there is a great need for thoughtful discussion of issues often thought to be too sensitive to deal with. There are, of course, many other issues worthy of discussion, such as the role of research in the under-graduate experience, the role of telecommunications, how best to teach science to nonscience majors, the internationalization of the curriculum, and so forth. I will deal here more directly only with the two often overlooked areas.

LIBERAL EDUCATION: AN OLD OR A NEW IDEA?

For almost two thousand years, liberal education as an ideal has attracted the attention and loyalty of thoughtful educators, schol-ars, and citizens concerned with higher education. Few educa-tional ideals have attracted more adherents, sustained more controversy, and had more "staying power" than this concept. For many centuries, educators, scholars, and citizens across a broad range of the political, social, and cultural spectrum have urged col-leges and universities to meet their civic responsibility of providing a curriculum that fulfills the imperatives of a liberal education.[14] This consistent devotion to an educational ideal is all the more remarkable given the enormous and continuing growth in our stock of knowledge, changing notions of what the word "liberal" implies, the ever-shifting nature of society's educational objectives, and the rather more startling fact that rarely has there been much agreement regarding what educational program or programs are included within the coveted label of "liberal education."[15]

The only organizing ideas that stand steady and clear over the past two millennia are that the aims of a liberal arts curriculum are to achieve important educational objectives complementary to

[14] Siegel, *Rhetoric and Philosophy in Renaissance Humanism*.
[15] I am indebted to Bruce A. Kimball's *Orators and Philosophers* (New York: College Board, 1995) and Oakley's *Community of Learning* for deepening my own understanding of these issues.

those of a purely technical or narrowly professional education (e.g., better understanding of our cultural inheritance, better understanding of oneself, an examination of the foundations of mathematics and science, clarification of what we mean by virtue) and to help create a certain type of citizen. In practice, of course, professional and liberal arts curricula certainly overlap, and notions regarding the "right" type of citizen are in a constant state of flux.

Even the Greeks, who are credited with discovering the basic components of the liberal arts, had several different educational strategies that focused variously on literature, the search for truth and new understanding, and the training of effective civic leaders. The articulation in Roman times of the *Septem Artes Liberales* (grammar, rhetoric, logic, arithmetic, geometry, music, and astronomy) did not lead, even at that moment, to the adoption by Roman educators of a coherent curriculum based on these subjects. Rather, Roman society included several approaches to higher education with greatly different emphases.

For Thomas Aquinas in late medieval Europe, a liberal education included, in addition to the *Septem Artes Liberales*, natural philosophy, moral philosophy, and metaphysics. As time passed, however, additional objectives for a liberal education were developed, such as the freeing of the individual from previous ideas, the disinterested search for truth, the pursuit of alternative ideas, and the development and integrity of the individual and of his or her power of reason. In many ways, of course, this expansion of the agenda of liberal education was a natural development as society's educational requirements expanded and evolved over time.

Thus, the classical societies of Greece and Rome, the European societies of the Renaissance, nineteenth-century Europe, and both colonial and contemporary America have all had their own quite distinct understandings of the purposes of a liberal education and/or of the role of higher education in achieving particular educational objectives. Not surprisingly, these tensions usually reflected quite disparate and contending social and cultural commitments (e.g., Hellenism versus Christianity, reason versus revelation) as well as distinct views of both the source of new wisdom and understanding and the role of institutions of higher education. The principal point is that although the concept of a liberal education goes back to classical times, so, too, does the controversy over its structure and purposes. Indeed, alternative approaches to a liberal education—in theory and practice—have been a constant source of tension in educational thinking for two millennia.

Despite this history of controversy, change, and evolution, the pursuit of this amorphous ideal remains an article of faith in much of higher education. This continuing "devotion" has been bought at a price, however; namely, we have continuously expanded the constellation of ideas the term "liberal education" accommodates. Thoughtful educators now use this venerable term to include everything from a narrow focus on the "old" or "new" canon of "great" texts to a serious study of any and all aspects of liberal arts subjects.[16]

The catalogue of liberal arts subjects is, of course, now greatly expanded beyond the trivium and quadrivium and includes all of the burgeoning sciences—although the incorporation of the theoretical and experimental sciences into a liberal arts curriculum remains incomplete in the sense that the literary and philosophical traditions still seem to hold a special stature. The label "liberal education" may cover educational curricula in which the institution prescribes students' choices, as well as curricula that

[16] We could substantially improve the debate surrounding the "great books" by using the adjective *wonderful*, which means full of wonder and perhaps awe, instead of *great*, a much cruder word. We have the Great Lakes, the Great War, the Great Leap Forward, the Great Unwashed, and so forth. Most often, this adjective is associated with big or massive and coarse emotions such as anger, pride, and courage. These are not good company for works of prose and poetry that are awe inspiring and/or add to our understanding of the human condition.

leave all such choice to the individual students. It incorporates all sorts of pedagogies that distribute responsibility and initiatives for learning in quite different ways between student and teacher. It embraces approaches ranging from those that emphasize breadth of knowledge to those that emphasize depth of understanding in a relatively narrow area.

Thus, while the concept of a liberal education continues to reign as an article of faith that seems to unite many of us, it often masks many important differences in educational philosophies and objectives. Perhaps our chief folly in all of this has been to shape our rhetoric as if there were no history of change and controversy on these issues and only one proper curriculum for everyone. There never has been a "right" curriculum, and, given rapidly changing circumstances and aspirations, the best we can hope for in the future is a continued exploration of the various possibilities.

CHARACTERISTICS OF A LIBERAL ARTS PROGRAM

No one should claim to have identified *the* most appropriate liberal arts program. Such agreement has never existed, even for brief moments of time in particular places. The best I can do is try to identify some characteristics of a liberal education that I believe are—for our time—very important.

My own prejudices are to associate a liberal education with the particular educational needs of contemporary Western liberal democracies. In this respect it is critical to remain cognizant of two characteristics of liberal democracies. First, we should recall, as Ernest Gellner has pointed out, how atypical it is to have sustained, over a number of centuries, a society with a great plurality of institutions that oppose and/or provide a balance to the power of the state.[17] Moreover, these institutions are protected and

[17] Ernest Gellner, *Conditions of Liberty* (New York: Viking Press, 1994).

often financially supported by the same state. The idea that the state could support institutions that prevent its own monopoly over power and truth from becoming too extreme is, in a historical sense, quite novel. In this situation it is essential not only to search continually for the right balance between constraining the state's power and authority yet enabling it to do its work but to find appropriate venues and programs for training a large cohort of thoughtful, responsible, and independently minded leaders capable of heading the multiple institutions that share power.

Second, although many would claim that the historical legacy of a liberal education emphasizes our common humanity rather than the unique needs of particular individuals or groups, the actual development of Western liberal democracies has granted increasing importance and recognition not only to the needs and desires of individuals and small family units but to the constantly escalating demands for group rights—demands that have made it increasingly difficult to attain the common agreements any coherent community requires. Both of these special conditions of Western liberal democracies require particular approaches to a liberal education.

So as to better understand ourselves and contemporary times, we need to discover and understand the great traditions of thought that have informed the minds, hearts, and deeds of those who came before us. After all, despite the distinctiveness of ourselves and our times, we are part of a larger and deeper stream of human experience. Our particular cultures may be only historical contingencies, but we ignore them at great peril to our continuing potential. Whatever the shortcomings of our predecessors—and there were many—and however limited the surviving remnants of their efforts, they remain a great source of inspiration and understanding as long as we do not deify any particular aspect of this valuable inheritance.

We must also free our minds and hearts from unexamined commitments (authority of all types) so as to consider new possibilities (including new "authorities") that might enhance both our own lives and—more broadly—the human condition and build our sympathetic understanding of others quite different from ourselves. In other words, we cannot allow freedom from authority to lead to excessive demands for individual gratification that are antisocial and leave no place for individual sacrifice for the common good.

A liberal education needs to prepare all thoughtful citizens for an independent and responsible life of choice that appreciates the connectedness of things and peoples. This involves the capacity to make moral and/or political choices that will give our individual and joint lives greater and more complete meaning, an understanding of how the world works, the capacity to distinguish between logical and illogical arguments, and an understanding of the inevitability of diversity. This is especially important in a world where individual responsibility and internal control are increasingly needed to replace and/or supplement the rigid kinship rules, strict religious precepts, and/or authoritarian rule that have traditionally served to order societies. It would also be helpful if a liberal education encouraged and enabled students to distinguish between self-interest and community interest, between sentimentality and careful thought, between learning and imagination, and between the power and limitations of knowledge.

These particular needs and/or criteria are very closely related to a set of notions and institutional arrangements I associate with liberal democracy. In particular, such an education would encourage both an empathetic understanding and a critical assessment of the different social arrangements and cultural experiences designed to give meaning to our individual and community lives. Thus, liberal education, like liberal politics, must be committed to tolerance and freedom and, to the greatest extent possible, be open to the broadest stream of human ideas and experience. But just as the radical idea of the completely neutral state is unattainable, so is a curriculum free of normative content, and just as a liberal democracy needs some notion of the good life to pursue, so a liberal education must be grounded in some educational commitments and values (e.g., tolerance and self-restraint).

In speaking either of liberal education or of liberal politics, it is necessary to distinguish between the ideal and its practice. A liberal education—despite its current aspirations to openness and inclusiveness—has often been an instrument of exclusion, well beyond the necessity imposed by the need to make some choices. The same is clearly true of liberal politics.

Both liberal politics and liberal education must be tempered by two critical understandings. First, the human condition—whatever we might wish—places some limit on the common agreements that can be reached by a group of citizens, however well meaning, with different ideas about what is most worthy. Inevitably, some voices may feel suppressed, since the values needed to ensure the survival of the enterprise altogether do not allow at the end of the day for the full expression of any and all sets of moral commitments. Consequently, liberal thought faces an inevitable tension between a commitment to tolerance and the liberty to pursue without restraint one's own individual identity, on the one hand, and the need to ensure the survival of the community and thus to maintain some restraints, on the other. Despite the hopes of the Enlightenment, voluntary consent, reason, and truth have not yet completely replaced coercion. I have no easy answer as to how to resolve these tensions. The best we can do is continue to explore the boundaries created by the issues that separate us.

The curricular criteria suggested above are tied to the fundamental liberal notions of the autonomy and importance of the individual and of finding new and better ways to respect differences and reject domination. This itself is not a commitment shared by everyone. For me, however, it remains—together with the judicial and political system and the many civic organizations designed to give it operational meaning—the greatest guarantee of our capacity to most fully realize and give sustained meaning to our human aspirations.

Looking Ahead: Moral Education

It is too soon to grasp the full meaning of the many astonishing developments with which the 1980s ended, including the startling political transformation of Eastern Europe and the former Soviet Union (and perhaps China), the internationalization of the world economies, the growth in population, the movement of peoples at unprecedented levels, and the establishment of worldwide information nets. There seems little question, however, that a global transformation of some sort is under way. These astonishing events—and others—have caused us to begin rethinking existing ideas and commitments across an ideological spectrum that runs from the bases of national polities to the possibilities of empire, from national security arrangements to the future role of tribal solidarity in international affairs, from the continuing viability of the idea of a nation to the meaning of socialism in an increasingly internationalized (transgovernment) economy, and from the meaning of individual freedoms to the bases of the moral commitments that create coherent communities. In America, for example, many are concerned that our social arrangements have resulted in too many Americans feeling disconnected from the country's future. Some thoughtful observers believe that our current policies, political arrangements, and social structure may not provide the cultural assets necessary for our continued cultural and economic vitality. At the very least, we seem to need a set of mobilizing beliefs and commitments and/or imagined objectives capable of fueling and refueling the individual and national effort as continued cultural vitality and national leadership require.

Recent events have led many to feel that our history, social institutions, and other cultural and economic arrangements still provide very uneven possibilities for different individuals and different groups—that our society is not really as open and equitable as we believed. This imbalance demands that we take a more critical look at the moral and political parameters of our traditions and institutions and the arrangements that distribute power and other benefits. Of particular concern are the principles, practices, and future of liberal democracies, the nation state, and the social contract that binds us to one another and to future generations.

If one needed any further evidence of the need for renewed thinking in these areas, one must only consider that liberal democratic values are being criticized for putting both too much and too little emphasis on the role of individual rights over the claims of tradition, social stability, and community. Symbolic of these uncertainties is the fact that in America the equal protection clause of the Constitution is now invoked to confer rights on virtually all persons who believe themselves excluded from certain benefits. Even the concept of diaspora, formerly connoting the despised, displaced, and disenfranchised, now rises from the ashes of history to present "imagined homelands" as a serious cultural ideal in an increasingly pluralistic world.

This general ferment bespeaks the search for a meaningful set of centering values and certainly will have implications for higher education, as do the ongoing changes in demographics, the nature and distribution of work, and attitudes toward government expenditures and taxes.

With respect to our undergraduate teaching programs, there is a widely perceived need, despite our overall success, to think more deeply about both teaching and the curriculum and to shift our priorities toward this particular social output of higher education. Many believe, for example, that faculty and administrators have become not only too "scattered" and specialized but too removed from the overall development of the student and not fully responsive to students' changing educational needs. Others believe the opposite, namely, that our teaching is not deep or demanding enough and that we pay too much attention to the developmental and social needs of students. It is a paradox why, in a highly competitive system, there remains an "inadequate" response to the claim that there is a great and unfulfilled demand for more and better teaching. Too often, we have confused issues of quality teaching with issues of curriculum. When thinking about these issues, one must distinguish between the "rightness" of procedures (i.e., the opportunities made available to and the choices made by students) and the "goodness" of outcomes (i.e., the nature of educated—degree-holding—people). The levers of educational policy operate only in the first area, although the hope is that the two areas are intimately related.

From many quarters in contemporary society, one senses an increased concern over the lack of principled and responsible behavior in both public and private life, particularly with respect to our communal obligations, the web of mutual obligations and understandings that should bind us together as a community. The sources of this concern, the examples of irresponsible and unprincipled behavior, both on and off campus, are only too easy to identify. For example, within academic communities, students, faculty, and administrators do not always exhibit a shared commitment to the values that sustain and enrich a community of learning, such as honesty, nonviolence, disinterestedness, the maintenance of thoughtful communication despite disagreement, and so forth. In a pluralistic, ethical world there will always be questions regarding whose moral values should dominate or just how we should take the various interests and commitments of "others" into account. One of the resulting issues for universities is the place of moral education in the university curriculum.

One aspect of a student's moral education lies not in the curriculum but in the behavior of the faculty, staff, and administration and in the policies of the institution. Students will observe how fairly and responsibly they are treated, what values are reflected in the university's rules and regulations and their administration, how the university treats its employees, how the university relates to the community, and how faithfully faculty and administrators keep their promises and defend the values of open and thoughtful debate that are central to a learning environment. How tolerant are they of others' views? How thoughtful is the feedback given to students? Is this feedback an exercise in judgment and honest criticism, or is it merely punitive in nature? Do faculty and administrators allow their individual liberty to overwhelm all other values? Do they shock and patronize students or awaken them? Do programs assist students in entering the world of internal speculation and reflective thought? Thoughtful observers—students and others—will discern if the university remains a symbol of enlightenment or an institution that identifies the good society with the status quo and special privileges.

One cannot avoid the question, however, as to the role of ethics in the curriculum, itself an issue of great uneasiness and disagreement. For the most part, the uneasiness stems from hesitancy to establish any particular moral orthodoxy. To put the matter simply, many faculty feel it is no longer appropriate for the institution to decide what ethics or whose ethics ought to be taught. This feeling is quite appropriate but need not—cannot—prevent universities from addressing the issue, since there are other avenues (direct or indirect) to moral education. If, for example, the university curriculum offered students an opportunity to develop their capacities to identify and analyze ethical issues, to understand that it is important to continue to discuss important moral issues even if we do not have a "ready answer," and to reinforce the spirit that we can learn from our disagreements in these matters, a great deal would be gained. If the university experience also helped convey the understanding that the capacity to choose is a critical aspect of being a moral person, a worthy objective would be achieved. If, in addition, the student begins to focus on which constraints he or she will choose to accept in making ethical choices, the university experience will have made a major contribution to students' moral education. Clearly, complex moral reasoning is not a substitute for moral behavior, but it is a beginning, and if the university experience unites this capacity with a commitment to democracy and concern for others throughout the institution, a great deal has been accomplished.

Since the founding of the American republic, there has been a constant level of anxiety concerning these issues. It has never been clear how to balance the tensions between biblical faith and rationalism (the scientific ethos), between pluralism and toleration, between self-interest and community interest, between individual liberty and communal values. At the moment, many wish to consider establishing a new balance between our commitments to individual liberty, private property, market competition, and due process on the one hand and self-restraint and communal concerns and obligations on the other. Many thoughtful observers seem to be searching for ways to reemphasize the latter set of concerns to halt what they perceive to be the increasing fragmentation of the social order.

In an earlier time a kind of moral consensus—defined by the trustees and president—was demanded of students and faculty alike. This was reassuring for many but provided little nourishment for the greater part of our national community, which was excluded. Although a return to the "good old days" is not recommended, there are valuable traditions and insights that we need to carry with us as we continue to address the moral issues of our own time.

The university should continue to play a role in helping us give our lives meaning and moral significance, in helping us understand the important contemporary lessons of "the golden rule" (taking other people's interests into account), and in teaching us to accept the inevitable anxiety that characterizes a moral and pluralistic society committed to democracy and change. Since we have chosen pluralism and representative government over other solutions such as official moral orthodoxies and/or totalitarianism, we face the special challenges (including political and social fragility) of any society that is not absolutely bound together by something akin to a dominant religion or strong kinship tradition.

The appropriate university response to the contemporary need for a greater sense of stability and moral significance in our lives must be different than in earlier years. It is the responsibility of the contemporary university to ensure that the great questions of human existence are before us for our students and faculty to wrestle with. Further, faculty, staff, and administrators must try to exhibit in both word and deed an exemplary commitment to ethically informed principles, and a commitment not only to their privileges but to their informing values and responsibilities.

I have sketched a journey over a rather broad historical landscape in order to emphasize several points. They might be summarized as follows:

- We have a great deal to learn from a more careful assessment of the historical evolution of higher education, but only if we avoid the utopian propaganda of educators (and the unthinking satire of others) and study the actual nature and meaning of classroom experience to students and faculty. There has long been a great chasm between aspirations and reality in undergraduate education.

- Despite the many contemporary challenges facing under-graduate education in America, the quality of the under-graduate experience has never been better.
- Aside from the question of the overall quality of secondary education, the chief obstacles to continued improvement in undergraduate education are the possibility that those in higher education will lose sight of this as their number-one quest and/or will resort to cultural "wars" rather than rational discourse over the issues of individualism and community, tradition and change, common cultural experiences and the reality of difference.
- It is once again necessary to rethink the nature and pur-pose of a liberal education and the nature of the univer-sity's responsibility for moral education.

All in all, the Western university has been a remarkably durable and adaptive institution. Although always the focus of criticism and some disappointment, these institutions have con-tinued to be valued by Western societies, sometimes as society's best hope for change and sometimes for reassurance regarding tra-ditional moral commitments. Notwithstanding the many revolutions that seem to characterize contemporary life—includ-ing the burgeoning of telecommunications; the development of a so-called politics of difference; the transformation of the nation state; the redistribution of people, capital, production facilities, and products around the earth's surface; and the perceived diminu-tion of moral certainties—it is unlikely that evolving events will bring about the demise of universities as we know them. Despite their many shortfalls, despite changing demographics, changing expectations, changing public and private priorities, despite a somewhat deteriorating physical infrastructure, and despite a sometimes shaken faith (both internal and external) in their potential civic contribution, these institutions will, once again, prove capable of adapting in a manner that reflects an understanding of the current environment.

There are few institutions with such continuing potential to deliver new social dividends to society, and, therefore, there is little reason to put them on the endangered species list. Universities may have to do with less, and they will certainly have to conduct a searching reexamination of their programs in the light of contemporary realities, but their unique potential for learning that centers around the power of the person-to-person encounter, their demonstrated capacity for largely peaceful interaction across many cultural divides, and their continuing ability to challenge the familiar will make them indispensable assets for the future as it unfolds.

CHAPTER 4

Graduate Students:
Too Many and Too Narrow?

Marye Anne Fox

D ISCUSSIONS CONCERNING WHAT constitutes
the optimal number of students in a graduate program are
usually raised in the context of economic stress and the difficulties
that new science, mathematics, and engineering graduates with
advanced degrees now face in finding suitable employment. This
situation has prompted high-level officials in the Clinton administration to characterize the underemployment of people with
Ph.Ds as one of the biggest social problems in the United States.

Although unemployment was low—about 1.6 percent—
among 1993 science, mathematics, and engineering graduates six
months after receiving their degrees, according to the most
recent survey of doctoral recipients,[1] even this figure was much
higher than the average in the previous decade. The same survey
also cites the rather stunning statistic that 50 percent of recent
graduates with bachelor's of science degrees in science and engineering are employed outside their fields and 24 percent of the

---

[1] *Science and Engineering Indicators* (Washington, D.C.: National Science
Foundation, 1996).

recipients of master's degrees in these areas are working outside their disciplines.

Furthermore, substantial anecdotal evidence indicates that many graduates who have found jobs believe they are underemployed (an additional 4.3 percent) in positions that neither require nor utilize the skills acquired through years of expensive education.[2] The sum of these numbers corresponds roughly to the current unemployment rate for the general population, making a lot of citizens, and some legislators, inquire whether the college experience is universally worthwhile.

How serious the unemployment or underemployment problem is varies by field, of course, but the pain associated with dashed expectations is clearly evident in discussions with recent graduates. In a letter to the editor of *Chemical and Engineering News*, for example, a recent graduate of a doctoral program in chemistry expressed clear personal trauma: "Jobs in chemistry are relatively scarce, low-paying, and unrewarding," he says, "and whether you're gifted or not doesn't matter. . . . Research doesn't pay on a quarterly basis, and it can't be justified by anyone wishing to climb the corporate ladder."

Potentially even more troubling is the pronounced effect of these unachieved dreams on the morale and aspirations of students who are now choosing career paths. Indeed, the nation has been particularly unsuccessful—despite major efforts at the National Science Foundation and other federal funding agencies—in motivating underrepresented groups, particularly members of racial minorities, to consider professional careers in science and engineering.[3]

If the driving force for this troubling situation is the dearth of secure employment opportunities in science and technology, it

[2] Ibid.
[3] Ibid.

would seem reasonable to ask potential employers for their opinions about the severity and expected duration of this problem. As a practicing chemist who frequently interacts with both academic and industrial scientists, I am in the position to do this. Thus, for three months in 1995, I conducted an informal opinion poll among my colleagues in industry on the question at hand: have the conditions in the United States changed so drastically that we should substantially cut back the size of our graduate programs and in so doing produce fewer scientists and engineers with Ph.D.s?

At the outset, one should recognize that chemistry is a field in which the range of possible employment options and career opportunities in education, in government, and in private industry has for a long time been recognized as being quite broad. It is probably one of the last fields in which employment difficulties should manifest themselves.

The group of more than fifty industrial chemists in my sample bifurcate into two camps. Without much hesitation, the members of one group say that the current slowdown is permanent, reflecting an evolutionary, paradigmatic change in the way technology will be developed, and that universities must make an immediate, substantial effort to reduce the number of students pursuing advanced training in science and engineering. In part because of the greatly enhanced productivity in science and engineering research that has been achieved over the past fifty years, it is now possible to do much more with many fewer hands, they are saying, and, as a result, universities must raise their admissions standards and concentrate on a small number of students who, with greatly increased productivity, can quite adequately provide the necessary innovation for the next century.

Members of the second group, with at least equal conviction, believe that the current slowdown is temporary and that as productivity in the United States improves and world markets are recovered, we will need more, not fewer, scientists and engineers with advanced training acquired in the same way that has proved to be so effective for the last thirty years. It is not so much that we are producing too many graduates, these industrial chemists argue, but that those now emerging from our colleges and universities are not trained broadly enough. They do not understand what is important in the commercial sector and are insufficiently creative, insufficiently entrepreneurial, and insufficiently sophisticated in the ways of the business world. These deficiencies are particularly apparent, the chemists say, in graduates of programs that lack a critical mass of talented student cohorts, of faculty experts, of state-of-the-art research equipment, and of financial support. The sentiments of this group of industrial chemists are also echoed among the first group, those who believe we should seriously reduce the size, and perhaps the number, of existing graduate programs.

WHAT IS SUFFICIENTLY BROAD TRAINING?

"What," I have asked in response, "would constitute sufficiently broad training?"

"Doctoral graduates need better communication skills," they reply, "verbal, written, and computational. They also need to be trained more broadly." (By this the responder usually means they should have additional coursework or practical experience in management, economics, the law, computer science, and so forth.) "They also must have mastered one technical subarea of their field and have demonstrated this mastery by publishing a record of their technical achievements in a refereed journal. And, by the way, it would be helpful if they would also have had at least one meaningful industrial internship and to have finished their entire graduate program in less than four years."

If one suggests that it just might be a little difficult to achieve all these objectives simultaneously and that choices would have to be made, the conversant will usually say, "It's not my place to tell universities how they should achieve their objectives."

This puts university decision makers in a position much like that of a young man in Eastern Europe soon after the ascendancy of communism who was confused about the meaning of dialectic materialism and consulted an elder rabbi in his village for help.

"Well, my son," said the rabbi, "suppose that while two men are working on a coal stove, it unfortunately blows out in one direction, spewing black smoke that completely covers the face of one of the workers but leaves the other untouched. Which of the two men will go to wash?"

"I suppose the one who is dirty," says the young man.

"No," says the rabbi. "The one with the dirty face will look at the man with the clean face and assume there is no need to wash. It is the man with the clean face who, recognizing what has happened to his friend, will go wash. Now, let us see how you have learned. I ask you again: suppose that while two men are working on a coal stove, it unfortunately blows out in one direction, spewing black smoke that completely covers the face of one of the workers but leaves the other untouched. Which of the two men will go to wash?"

"Ah," says the student, "the man with the clean face will go wash."

"No," says the rabbi, "the man with the clean face will look at the man with the dirty face, will wipe his face with his hand, and, seeing no soot, will be thankful that he has escaped, whereas the man with the dirty face, on wiping his face, will see that he must go wash."

"But, rabbi," says the student, "this is the opposite conclusion you reached earlier for the same situation."

"Now you can understand the virtue of dialectic materialism," says the rabbi. "No matter how you answer, you are bound to be wrong."

In that spirit I continue, for university administrators are virtually never deterred by the possibility that anything they say on a given topic is likely to be wrong. Even so, I offer my ideas on graduate programs with a fair amount of trepidation and wariness. In doing so, I will bypass a closely related question: namely, the appropriate number of foreign-born graduate students that should be supported from U.S. resources. This is a complex question, especially in those fields in which native-born American students are in short supply. I will therefore make suggestions only about the kind of education we offer students who are reasonably committed to joining the American workforce, in a variety of capacities, upon completion of their graduate studies.

The question of what constitutes the appropriate size of graduate programs must be posed in a much broader context, one in which the very missions and character of the U.S. research university are being challenged. The current degree of introspection and reexamination of widely held tenets, of bold anti-intellectual challenges of our most dearly held assumptions, are unprecedented in post–World War II Western nations. Deconstructionists, moreover, tell us that there are no physical truths, that an equally valid, alternate science may have developed had we begun with an arbitrarily different set of physical postulates.

New Ways of Learning, New Career Paths

At the same time, the recent technological developments of electronic networking and telecommunication have made possible distance learning and new modes of information transfer that only recently were the stuff of science fiction. To many Americans, university professors are regarded as more fungible and more expendable, certainly less of a national treasure, than when I was a student. The new transferability of knowledge has altered the very definition of education.

Recently, the Department of Labor has projected that the average American college graduate of today will change careers—not just employers—about five times during his or her work life. This means, for example, that a well-trained chemist hired this year by a Dow or a Du Pont might be called upon to work at the bench (or at the synchrotron or at the supercomputer) synthesizing and characterizing a new polymer before she moves into middle management and deals with personnel and diversity issues, before she directs a program on economic analysis and risk assessment in cooperation with a corporate legal department, before she acts as a corporate liaison with unions and community workers and then ends up as a corporate vice president for business affairs or, better perhaps, as a secondary school teacher.

Reviewing the list of courses in which such a student might have enrolled at the graduate or undergraduate level, one might have trouble finding a match with the job skills this new graduate will ultimately need. Is a second semester of quantum mechanics really important as a basis for constructing a business plan? Without much work, it is easy to convince oneself that no matter what sequence of courses one might have required of such a student, one could not have anticipated all of her needed capabilities, much less those of her lab partner, who might follow a completely different career path from the same core learning experience.

More than ever our colleges and universities must be places where students can learn how to learn, not places where a set of temporally fixed data is transferred from a well-meaning professorial talking head to a meek and polite student sponge. Universities are not, and never have been, trade schools. The need to emphasize the habit of learning rather than the content of a curriculum is not new: this approach was taken by the ancient Greeks and even has its origin in the meaning of the word *education*, "to draw out."

We have known for a long time how advanced students can learn with exquisite facility to conduct the wonderful work of science and engineering. Universities do what the medieval guilds did so effectively: they apprentice their students to masters who personally push and pull, cajole and praise, until the apprentice can function independently as a master on his own. In the 1950s, immediately after the foundation of the National Science Foundation, this process used to take three or four years; now it typically takes five or six. Still, the dramatic discoveries and the personal developmental successes born from the core research group in the modern research-intensive university attest to the excellence and effectiveness of this pathway.

We know that the student must immerse himself or herself wholeheartedly in the methodology, in the literature, in the culture of the discipline if he or she is to contribute to the knowledge base and to master the scientific method. Because the student must taste the sweet fruit of discovery based on hypothesis and exploration, this immersion must be long enough for him or her to pose and solve a significant problem. Having done so, the student will have learned an area in great depth and will be in a position to make substantive contributions to basic research in the chosen subarea. If the research group and the mentor interact effectively, the student will know both how to work in a team and how to communicate clearly in oral and in written form.

This method simultaneously produces a well-trained scientist or engineer and new knowledge that can be transferred either in the flesh of the newly hired student or through the published literature, in books, journals, or patents. This method provides a cadre of experts who develop new technology in industry and ask important knowledge-based questions in our best institutions of higher learning. These are the ways by which new knowledge is uncovered and by which technology is transferred to the producers, to those who make the goods our society needs.

This technology is the basis of much of our national prosperity and is responsible for our steadily improving quality of life.

There is an apparent and indisputable need for a continuing complement of students trained in just this way. It is these students who, while working in a chosen discipline, will push back the frontiers of knowledge and create entirely new areas for exploration and investigation. Their contributions are clearly indispensable to a society that values innovation.

PROBLEMS WITH THE TRADITIONAL APPROACH

There is a down side to this method, however, if this route is to be used for all students. The first concern underlying this approach is the implicit assumption that each student is research driven and will employ the methodology of exploratory research as his or her single career path. In fact, many students pursue the Ph.D. degree mainly as a credential, rather than as the first step in a continuing commitment to scientific discovery. For them, it may be that the usual period expected for completion of a dissertation may involve a greater-than-necessary commitment of resources.

In some cases, students may consider the completion of a research-intensive Ph.D. degree a necessary ticket that will enable them to qualify for but quickly escape from a job in an industrial research lab into the ranks of corporate management. Or will a fourth, fifth, or sixth year of working with, say, the physical interactions transpiring within molecular beams really improve the quality of performance of the student who hopes to teach in a small liberal arts college or in a community college? When it comes to graduate programs, one size, unfortunately, does not necessarily fit all.

The second concern is related to the fact that the U.S. system of financial support for academic research appropriately focuses on peer-reviewed individual projects. This requires the master—the mentor—to be creative and to explore new directions within a defined sphere, but it does not require the apprentice to examine whether the same sphere will apply to his or her professional work. It does not make it clear that direct cloning of the master is not mandatory and may not even be desirable.

These two problems create a dilemma for a research mentor dealing with a group of students with a range of aspirations. Somehow we must convey to our students that change, or flux, is an opportunity, not a condemnation, and that the nation has a pressing need for technically literate people with a variety of backgrounds; that one can be a success in life without being a tenured faculty member or a university-based research scientist; that the skills learned in a graduate research program are transferable to other important environments; that creativity and discovery—personal renewal—can flourish outside the academic or corporate laboratory; and that a new graduate who has followed his or her interests should be sufficiently self-confident to embrace uncharted routes and undefined opportunities beyond the duplication of his or her current position.

When the academy fails to teach learning to learn as the goal of higher education, it cheats at least some of its students, who erroneously accept the premise that their highest intellectual goal is to become a replica of their teacher. Such graduates reproduce their teachers' jobs, and often their professors' own thesis research problems, in a new environment, striving under adverse circumstances to come up with incremental advances. Such replication is tolerable when what is needed is geometric expansion of the personnel working in a given area; it fails miserably when there is a flat or declining academic base.

It is this inability of some students to picture a dynamic, evolving career path for themselves outside a university that has contributed to the proliferation of graduate programs at second- and third-tier institutions. Often lacking a critical mass of bright and dedicated students as well as the necessary breadth of offerings to provide the means for broad-based learning to learn, these graduate programs do a disservice to the faculty and to the students who join them so that only infrequently are both programmatic goals and student aspirations achieved.

If we are to avoid this trap, our faculty must accept that not every graduate student, even if very bright, should work diligently at the academic bench for five or six years before moving to a post-doctoral position at another academic bench for another two to three years. Some students will, of course, follow just that path, but others, who are at least as bright and as useful to our society, need not do so. Our faculty must offer sufficient curricular flexibility to encourage at least some of our apprentices in science and engineering to develop other, less research-driven skills. This would provide an appealing alternative career path for those who can, and will, do research to meet degree requirements but who do not love it, who lack the zeal, the fire in the belly, characteristic of most researchers who will make revolutionary breakthroughs in science and engineering. And it would use the impressive skills of these highly talented students much more productively.

Alternatives to Traditional Graduate Programs

Imagine, if you will, a university in which some of the doctoral students would demonstrate complete familiarity with the tenets of a discipline, perhaps by completion of a program of work at least as deep as now required for a master's degree. Students might then choose one or even two other fields into which their newly acquired research skills might be tried under the supervision of an adviser or group. With the direction of an active faculty mentor as coordinator, an initial intense reading period in the second or third field could be followed by a research project of defined scope in which the students would develop new knowledge of a quality appropriate for professional publication. The unifying knowledge gained in these disparate investigations would be the students' (not the mentors'), and the preparation of a dissertation relating the various investigations would be the culminating experience of the degree program. The final examination would be a truly interdisciplinary feast. The possible combinations are endless: perhaps a pharmacy program combined with work in organic synthesis and in medical economics; a program in high-energy physics combined with work in the social implications of energy policy; or a program in molecular biology combined with work in epidemiology and education.

With this approach, we must ask whether the scientific method and the techniques of research might not be learned within a shorter period by students who do not intend to specialize in hands-on research and whether what we currently call a master's program, when combined with a business or law or psychology research experience, might better prepare some students for the circuitous career paths they may ultimately follow. With this approach, some students may even choose to learn skills off campus in for-profit research venues. Responsible mentors will have to familiarize themselves with the intellectual vitality of these nonacademic endeavors.

PROVIDING GUIDANCE AND OPTIONS

Some will say that students have these options now. But do universities really accept such students and provide them with sufficient guidance about their aspirations? Do they assure them, clearly and explicitly, that there are many valuable career options that depend on a strong technical background without focusing on research? If universities do not, should we be surprised when students do not accept such paths and are not open to the nonresearch-intensive possibilities that present themselves when they move on? Should we be surprised that some students leave our universities with unrealistic career aspirations that can lead to low job satisfaction?

Does this approach mean there will be fewer graduate students? Not really. For every student who chooses to reduce the fraction of scholarly graduate work done at the academic bench, other students who currently are unable to incorporate such experiences into their graduate studies may find it attractive to include a year or two of in-depth research work into their programs. Consider who would be better educated and more employable: a patent attorney who has or has not had an inventive laboratory experience; a journalist specializing in environmental regulation who has or has not worked in developing new methods of trace analysis or in conducting an ecological survey; a judge who has or has not actually run an electrophoretic gel to analyze and characterize DNA.

In this operational mode, the weakness of second- and third-tier institutions would also be more obvious to students who wish to partake of a wider range of options, and it might accelerate what may well be the inevitable shrinking—perhaps even the demise—of weak Ph.D.-granting programs, making it possible for such institutions to better use their resources to improve the quality of undergraduate instruction.

What would be required to implement such options within our current university infrastructure? Several nontrivial attitudinal and curricular changes would be needed. First, prospective students would need to have a broader undergraduate education to ensure that they are adequately prepared to benefit from interdisciplinary experiences and have the skills and self-confidence to learn the basic skills of another discipline through dedicated reading.

Second, a substantial fraction of the active research faculty in many disciplines would have to be willing to devise intellectually challenging projects that can be accomplished within a year or two; that is, they would have to be willing to make a major commitment to providing a coordinated framework within which the shorter projects could be integrated into a truly significant program and to team students in abbreviated programs with other members of the research group who have longer-term commitments to the general project goals.

Third, prospective employers (in the academy, in the government, and in the private sector) would have to be willing to accept degrees with strange, or in some cases unique, names (perhaps technology transfer or environmental ecology, rather than physics, biology, or civil engineering) and to be sufficiently openminded to evaluate the entire portfolio of a graduate program rather than searching only for demonstration of in-depth competence in a narrowly defined area.

Given the magnitude of the changes required, it is easy to see why this proposal would be difficult to implement, especially on a short time scale, and why many students, probably most, would continue to elect a traditional in-depth research experience for their graduate work. If universities encourage such flexibility in graduate education for some graduate students, who will do the work now done by teaching assistants? Who will populate basic research laboratories? Initially, there might be little change, as most students would matriculate in a departmental program central to their individual program, and many would be supported, as they are now, as they undertake coursework during the first year relevant to their chosen goals.

In subsequent years of study, however, a wider percentage of university students would be incorporated into the flexible program, including those who aim to partake of an academic experience as one of their life works, perhaps as part of a graduate experience or as part of a collaborative scholarly project being pursued with a faculty member and focusing on new learning methods. Or perhaps the tasks done by teaching assistants and researchers in basic laboratories would be undertaken by appropriately paid postdoctoral colleagues working in both teaching and research capacities with continuing appointments. This approach would demand—and would likely produce—higher-quality under-graduate instruction, which is surely the rightful expectation of students and parents who are paying a lot for such expertise, in that these duties would be the essence of the paid position, not imposed tasks that interfere with the real business at hand.

Whether such options could become reality is surely conjec-tural. But as educators dream, or at least wander about the new infrastructural terrain of the evolving university, perhaps they should not even think about whether there should be fewer grad-uate students but rather how to provide a new continuum of options for graduate and postgraduate programs.

CHAPTER 5

Prospect for the Humanities

Hanna H. Gray

CRITICS THROUGHOUT THE academic world mourn what they see as the disintegration of the humanities at the core of a liberal education and fear that the prospects for genuine scholarship have been irreversibly eroded. On the defensive both within and outside the academy, humanists are blamed for the failings of education and for the ills of a culture said to be declining and dissolving. They believe that they have lost ground and priority to other fields, feel constrained by the decrease in opportunities in the academic world, and are anxious about the sustenance of humanistic learning and its institutions.

NATURE OF THE CRISIS

The humanities make up a divided universe, rent by hotly contested differences over their identity and purpose and over the forms of knowledge and of knowing or thinking about knowing that give dignity to humanistic scholarship and education. The sense of crisis in education and of crisis in the humanities go hand in hand, for to think about the purpose and possibilities of the one is to declare a position on the other. Every humanism has at its heart a vision and a program of education. Every stated goal of liberal learning and every curriculum depend on a conception of the civilizing and enabling consequences—private and public, social and cultural—that educated people may experience and contribute, as on a conception of what should characterize a genuinely educated person. These depend on some deeply held views, perhaps utopian but in any case exemplary, of human capacity and potential projected into a future toward which we are urged to aspire.

Although many of the controversies swirling about the humanities are taking place within the academy and its haunts, there are also troublesome signs of a growing or at least increasingly explicit gap or asymmetry between the work of academic humanists and the expectations or understandings of the larger public. Humanists are being charged with speaking arcane languages, pursuing narrower specializations, and seeking sanctuary within the university to carry on campaigns of scholarly irrelevance and political indoctrination. The notion transmitted and reinforced in the general public is that literature is no longer concerned with great writing, history with significant events, philosophy with important ideas, or any of these disciplines with rigorous standards of scholarship, objective analysis, or a just appreciation and sense of the past. The fear is that politics has become the aim, politicization the means, political correctness the orthodoxy, and nihilism the epistemology of the humanities in our time. In short, a concern has emerged that education has become trivialized and enervated, standards erased, and the foundation for breadth debased.

In their defense, humanists assert that they are waging a campaign against another deeply ingrained and manipulative political correctness—the dominant orthodoxies of the powerful and the entrenched interests of those who fear intellectuals and their critical stance. This correctness, humanists say, holds sway and has long held sway in our society.

Symptoms of the Gap between Humanists and the Public

The charges and countercharges that followed the publication of the "national standards" for history in schools are but one reflection of this mutual alienation. Yet another acute symptom of the gap between humanists and the public can be seen in the heated discussion surrounding the future of the National Endowment for the Humanities (NEH). The prospect that it may disappear, the belief that the voices raised on its behalf are muffled and lost in the wilderness of indifference and hostility to what humanists care for and strive to accomplish, the conviction that support for the NEH is *the* essential means, both symbolic and material, by which the larger society may express or repudiate any concern for the humanities and their worth, all this has led those fearful of its abolition to equate the future of the humanities with the future of the NEH itself.

Most people in the academy want the NEH to survive and would say it has done much good for humanistic scholarship. At the same time, humanistic scholarship, education, and culture would survive the demise of such public funding, despite the more straitened circumstances, and would survive in ways that many fields of science could not survive the disappearance of the National Science Foundation or of the National Institutes of Health, for example. To say this is not to devalue the humanities or to subordinate them to other fields in the hierarchy of academic value, or to believe that our society is incapable of caring for the role that humanistic learning might play. Yet all these assertions have been made, and that underscores the sad uncertainty afflicting the humanistic enterprise.

ROOTS OF THE "CRISIS"

Thirty years ago, when the endowments were born, a commission
under the auspices of the American Council of Learned Societies
argued the case for the humanities as being in the national interest, as having civic purposes. The humanities, it was said, were in
crisis. Science had prospered; what was needed was an improved
balance, the restoration of the faltering and starved humanities.[1]

Two points are important here. First, the humanities seem
always to be in crisis. This is perhaps the natural state of studies
and reflections that look to the most difficult questions of the
human condition and its meaning. The humanities have, after
all, to do with the worlds of history and human expression, with
the struggle toward illumination and judgment in the midst of
complexity and contingency, with problems of value and choice,
of knowledge and diverse methods of knowing in matters that
are ambiguous, often paradoxical, and rarely susceptible to clear-
cut solutions.

Fifteen years after the endowments came into being, yet
another commission on the humanities, this one sponsored by the
Rockefeller Foundation, painted a still bleaker picture. It concluded that the humanities were "in grave crisis" and their decline
a sign of "the general weakening of our vision and resolve."[2] This
phrase actually repeated the words of the 1964 commission, which
had said that the challenge to the weakened humanities had to be
met with "vision and resolve"—that is, by creating the endowment.

In the ensuing years we have seen not just the blandly elevated
rhetoric of commissions and committees but best-selling books
and many manifestos anything but bland take up the charge and

[1] *Report of the Commission on the Humanities* (New York: American Council of
Learned Societies, 1964), 1–8.
[2] *The Humanities in American Life: Report of the Commission on the Humanities*
(Berkeley and Los Angeles: University of California Press, 1980), 3.

raise the specter of the imminent end of civilization as reflected in the crisis of the humanities. A colleague remarked about one of their authors, a former chairman of the National Endowment of the Humanities, "The man has a special gift—difficult to describe, a kind of negative charisma, an ability to give a bad name to eternal truths."[3]

Second, Americans have always been skeptical about the value of the humanities to education and to life. Or they have made a sharp demarcation between universities, where such matters get some attention, and life, where the real world takes hold and serious problems require full attention.

Many pious suggestions have been made that the humanities may be useful in enhancing the quality of life, as a kind of amenity. Others, however, feel that they may be directly useful to people engaged in the world's affairs. For instance, a publisher's ad for an anthology called *The Classic Touch* begins:

> Since practicing managers rarely have the time to read or reread the classics in their entirety, the authors of *The Classic Touch* have put together a treasure trove of passages and stories that resonate with meaning for the task of management in the modern world. This captivating collection includes selections from Plato's *Republic*, the best text ever written on leadership style; Miller's *Death of Salesman*, on the care and feeding of a sales force; Thoreau's *Walden*, on the badness of bigness; Shakespeare's *King Lear*, a drama of succession, delegation, and decentralization; and Homer's *Iliad*, a rich commentary on motivation and communication.

---

[3] Stuart Tave, "Words, Universities, and Other Odd Mixtures," Ryerson Lecture, University of Chicago, April 3, 1991.

The promotional materials go on to say that "*The Classic Touch* talks to managers who want to know more than the formulas and techniques of accounting, marketing, production and computers, managers who know that their work is really creative, their accomplishments truly heroic. It is a practical book, for anyone who loves to hear a valuable lesson entertainingly taught." Clearly, in the game of arming and aiming the "canon," people can shoot themselves in the foot.

The romance of the humanities always captivated the earnest and idealist side of our national psyche. There is also a long and wonderful tradition of looking to the humanities for serious solutions. This is the tradition that leads people to go to classes at 10 o'clock at night so they can read the great books in their entirety.

Alexis de Tocqueville summarized the tension that has haunted higher learning in America when he asked whether the democratic ethos can be consistent with what we might call the quest for fundamental knowledge, more particularly, an immersion in intellectual activity and reflection. So, too, his warning, which could be a kind of credo for our universities. He wrote, "If the light by which we are guided is ever extinguished, it will dwindle by degrees and expire of itself. By dint of close adherence to mere applications, principles would be lost sight of, and when the principles were wholly forgotten, the methods could no longer be invented, and men would continue without intelligence and without art to apply learned processes no longer understood."[4]

Throughout our history there runs the deep recurrent resonance of multiple strains of populism and anti-intellectualism, of an emphasis on the visibly and usefully practical, whether for the purposes of professional life or for the advancement of the social good. Accompanying these themes are the equally varied and

[4] Alexis de Tocqueville, *Democracy in America*, ed. Philips Bradley (New York: Knopf, 1964), 2:47.

clamorous fears associated with the critical and questioning spirit that lies at the heart of a commitment to learning and its consequences. All of these strains have had major effects on the development and status of our universities themselves, of course—on the demands made on them, on the expectations surrounding the education they should provide, on the environment in which they participate.

The word *academic* in our world has lots of connotations, rarely positive. It rouses a whole range of reactions, from mild suspicion to not always affectionate laughter; there are the mere academic, the dry-as-dust academic, the head-in-the-clouds academic, the pedant academic, the hypocrite academic, and even, of course, the dangerously academic. Academics themselves often take a dim few of their own. One symbol of that is Moses Hadas's memorable one-line book review of a scholarly monograph. "This book," he wrote, "fills a much needed gap."

It is of some significance that such views of the academic are by no means confined to the world outside the academy. From the late nineteenth century and ever after, there occurred fierce debates on the relative positions of science and the humanities in the work of education and research, together with intense arguments over the comparative weight that should be assigned to them. The driving guidelines and models for the idea of research, whatever the field, were after all meant to be scientific, empirical, investigatory, ultimately professional and disciplinary, critical, and imbued with a spirit of building the structures of objective knowledge. To some extent these standards and aspirations had already transformed humanistic study, if not in the collegiate curriculum, then surely in the work of scholarship.

In the new universities the organization of departments and graduate study and growing specialization swept through the humanities as well as the sciences. But there existed those who lamented these developments as threatening to kill the spirit, as inimical to the vision of humanistic culture that looked to large goals of enrichment and appreciation, to the sustenance of the past and its legacies for the present and future, in disseminating those civilizing values by which they hoped the lives of individuals and communities would be strengthened. And there were always those who feared that this vision was put at risk by the claims and imperial designs of other disciplines and other intellectual priorities, who saw in the academicization of humane learning a path to its inevitable distortion and waning and who feared that the prospects for genuine education and thus for universities were increasingly impoverished.

Our universities and their publics have witnessed over and over again these passionate conflicts, which in turn have animated the debates over education and its purposes, the knowledge most worth having and its uses. We have seen wave after wave of such discussion. At present it looks like a really big wave—a surfer's wave.

Over this time, the disciplines themselves have undergone significant transformation; one can see that in the whole range of the humanities. The obvious point is that the boundaries and configurations, the content and ruling perspectives of the academic and disciplinary landscape, have shifted, and they will always shift over time, even while the names and organizational forms that define that universe may abide. It is perhaps useful to emphasize how permeable have become once-rigid lines as demonstrated in particular by the close ties between scholars identified with critical theory and cultural studies on either side of what was once a much greater divide between the humanities and social sciences.

Defining the Traditions in the Humanities

As these shifts in intellectual direction take hold and as the universe covered by the term "humanities" becomes more crowded, complex, and diverse, it becomes more difficult again to define the humanities themselves. As humanists have done battle with one another, and have felt themselves embattled in their institutions and in the larger world, they have found any consensus on that question harder to achieve. Whether the humanities be conceived as a form of knowing, as a set of disciplines, of methodologies, or of scholarly and educational purposes, or as a way of thinking about and seeing the world, its achievements and possibilities, its questions and dilemmas, any assessment of the prospects for the role of humanistic scholarship and the breadth of liberal education in our universities must come to terms with the implications contained in these issues.

Universities have the dual function of conserving, renewing, and rethinking knowledge of the past and its inherited traditions, while at the same time questioning the ideas and the assumptions that are taken for granted and engaging in the potentially innovative work of new discovery and fresh, often revisionist, interpretation. Universities exist in part to maintain and nurture fields and ways of thinking that may not ever be fashionable but that are of fundamental importance—Sanskrit, for example—because they are important. Simultaneously, they exist to encourage and enable the intellectual freedom and risk taking that open up new problems and answers and arguments, whatever pain may follow in their wake. In this delicate and imperfect calibration, there have been instances of lost causes and trendy errors, as there have been many episodes of inbred resistance to the intellectually innovative and impatient disregard for the continuing vitality of the substantive accomplishment of predecessors.

The rhythm of the humanities has seemed to correspond to a pattern long ago observed by Alfred North Whitehead, who wrote, "Every intellectual revolution which has ever stirred humanity into greatness has been a passionate protest against inert ideas. Then alas, it has proceeded by some educational scheme to bind humanity afresh with inert ideas of its own fashion."[5]

It sometimes seems as though there was too little left for textual scholars to do. Humanistic scholarship has suffered from too close an analogy to the scientific model and as a result has seemed sometimes to become a parody of that. John R. Searle has written,

> The absence of an accepted educational mission in many literary studies has created a vacuum waiting to be filled. Perhaps the original mistake was in supposing that there is a well-defined academic discipline of literary criticism, as opposed to literary scholarship, capable of accommodating Ph.D. programs, research projects, and careers for the ambitious. When such a discipline fails to be "scientific" or rigorous, or even well defined, the field is left wide open for various fashions such as deconstruction or for the current political enthusiasms."[6]

We can see something of what Searle is talking about in the special vocabularies and scholastic methods attached to the activity that claims to be a discipline of literary criticism even while its adherents maintain that there can be no certainty in the elucidation of textual meanings or any certainty of judgment as to the relative qualities of texts. Such epistemologies, in turn, while stating that language is arbitrary and culture the reflection of power and the relationships of power, appear to assert at once a radical relativism and the teaching that language can nonetheless communicate these truths as true in fact. That, finally, generally

---

[5] Alfred North Whitehead, *The Aims of Education* (1928; reprint, New York: Free Press, 1967), 97-98.

[6] John R. Searle, "The Storm over the University," *New York Review of Books,* Dec. 6, 1990, 38.

coincides with an intellectual program highly and consciously political in outlook. To paraphrase John Searle again: "It confuses the unsurprising discovery that there is a political element in almost everything with the reductionist conclusion that everything is political."[7]

This program advocates a liberation from tradition through the unmasking of tradition, as though tradition were a given rather than a continually reappropriated and reconfigured source and object of reflection. Tradition in this agenda evokes the dominating, even oppressive Eurocentric culture reflected in the literary canons, historical myths, philosophical biases, and sociopolitical principles otherwise known as Western civilization. It is exclusive rather than inclusive, falsely hierarchical, and deliberately coercive. Yet, paradoxically, the schools and shades of thought I have characterized much too simplistically are skeptical of the word even while asserting its power and similarly skeptical of tradition even while extending and enlarging it.

But tradition is not a static inheritance passed on through a chain of letters. The leading question posed by and for the humanities is in some sense always "What is our tradition?" "What is our history?" To argue that it is not what we thought it was is to call on its own driving impulses. To say it should not be unthinkingly accepted is to rethink and perhaps to enrich it, as has so much of the new scholarship, as has so much of the work of literary criticism.

It is important to remind ourselves of the assumptions that have shaped the study of the humanities and our tradition. It is a tradition of criticism, rather proudly subversive and antiauthoritarian in outlook. It is intensely self-critical and intensely self-conscious. It is characteristically interested in other cultures in part as a way of defining itself.

---

[7] Searle, "Is There a Crisis in American Higher Education?" *Bulletin of the American Academy of Arts and Sciences* 46 (Jan. 1993): 39.

The idea of "Eurocentrism" and the questioning of "Euro-centrism," as well as the interest in the comparative study of civilizations, sprang to life with the discovery of the new world in the sixteenth century. It is a tradition that is sought in history, in its products, and in the development of a historical sensibility, not dogmas to be accepted but participation in a dialogue, an ancient and ongoing dialogue of sharply diverging voices. It is a tradition that has placed the highest value on intellectual free-dom while insisting on the requirements of a responsible intel-lectual integrity.

The old radical conservative Irving Howe once wrote of the excitement of his student days at the City College of New York:

> Knowledge of the past, we felt, could humanize by pro-moting distance from ourselves and our narrow habits, and this could promote critical thought. Even partly to grasp a significant experience or literary work of the past would require historical imagination, a sense of other times, which entail moral imagination, a sense of other ways. It would create a kinship with those who would come before us, hoping and suffering as we have, seeking through language, sound and color to leave behind some-thing of enduring value.

He went on to say:

> The past is the substance out of which the present has been formed, and to let it slip away from us is to acquiesce in the thinness that characterizes so much of our culture. Serious education must assume in part an adversarial stance toward the very society that sustains it—a democ-ratic society makes the wager that it is worth supporting a culture of criticism. But if that criticism loses touch

with the heritage of the past, it becomes weightless, a mere compendium of momentary complaints.[8]

The prospects for the humanities in our universities depend on a restless, inquiring, reflective, steadfast commitment to just that spirit and its search for the leap of critical imagination in the work of education and scholarship. Our universities will offer that kind of home to the humanities if they insist on a principled refusal to teach or to tolerate what someone once called "cheap and simple interpretations of life and of history." They must be places with an extraordinary tolerance for diverse views of the humanities, diverse understandings of the questions that they ask. They must also be institutions that are willing to set some standards of quality, that are unwilling to be used for purposes that are not their own, that are unwilling ever to compromise with shoddiness.

In short, the universities will be homes and enabling homes for the humanities if they are faithful to their own mission. Will it happen? Can it be? Of course it can.

[8] Irving Howe, "The Value of the Canon," *New Republic*, Feb. 18, 1991, 42, 43.

CHAPTER 6

Prospect for
Science and Technology

Neal Lane

IN 1946, JOHN MASEFIELD, an English poet laureate, said, "There are few things more enduring than a university."[1] Many people seemed to agree, for several decades followed during which universities were the routine recipients of the federal government's largesse and the nation's praise.

For the research university to remain a national treasure, however, it must have a prescription for addressing the impending downturn in federal funds. In short, it must find ways to do more with less. This will require real change for universities and for the National Science Foundation (NSF). What is necessary is for a stronger link to be created between scientific research institutions and society so that research is deemed to be more effective and benefits people more visibly.

Somehow, we in the research community must make better connections with the society beyond our laboratory walls. We should strive to overcome the traditional barriers that have sepa-

[1] John Masefield, speech, June 25, 1946, University of Sheffield.

rated disciplines by fostering cooperation not competition. We must throw away antiquated and artificial notions of applied and basic research that have served to divide researchers and that inhibit connections from being made between research and societal needs. And we must focus more sharply on making critical connections between our performance as researchers and our performance as teachers.

CONNECTIONS BETWEEN SCIENCE AND SOCIETY

There was a time when training in the sciences was an integral component of the education of a poet, a philosopher, or a historian—and a time when the scientist was also a poet, a philosopher, or a historian. As society advanced and entrenched, science became separated from history, literature, and philosophy—until C. P. Snow labeled scientists and engineers a separate culture from humanists.[2] More serious today is the separation, real and perceived, of science from society itself.

This separation, which reflects both isolation and autonomy, nullifies a great many contributions that scientists can make to furthering larger societal goals. It also appears to exonerate them from many of their responsibilities in society. To put it a bit too simply, scientists' contributions and opinions are not as widely sought and credited as they should be. And, likewise, scientists are not as ready to offer their services to society as perhaps would be ideal.

Science is ever more connected to life on the planet today and our world very much predicated on and powered by science and technology. Anyone who has sent an e:mail message or used the World Wide Web or even gone through a checkout line can attest to the rapid effects science can have on our daily routines.

[2] C. P. Snow, *The Two Cultures* (Cambridge: Cambridge University Press, 1959).

Thus, scientists cannot afford to hold science separate and autonomous from our everyday lives. Our nation, indeed every society, and its people have real needs and problems. Science must toil as a partner in finding solutions. And to be fully credible, the science community will have to better reflect the rich diversity of society as a whole.

There are notable examples of scientists and institutions that have close connections with the people on the receiving end of research; however, the research community has generally lived an independent and somewhat isolated existence within American society. That is no longer tenable. Informed debate on public policy, high-value jobs, competition in global markets, and the education of current and future generations require that science become a more integral part of our national fabric. This does not mean that basic research will be any less important in the future than it has been in the past. But it does imply some change in behavior, in values, and in focus.

Bertrand Russell once noted that "Da Vinci was equally pre-eminent in art and science, but it was from his art that he derived his greatest fame."[3] Modern society has grown to recognize and value its scientists as well as its artists. But along with that recognition come increased expectations of performance and accountability. Scientists must be prepared to be tested in ways they have not been in the past.

CONNECTIONS BETWEEN DISCIPLINES

The versatility of Leonardo leads naturally to my next topic: the connections between scientific disciplines. Discussion of fields

[3] Bertrand Russell, "Science to Save Us from Science," *New York Times Magazine*, March 19, 1950.

that are often treated as separate and distinct is vital if those in the university community are to overcome the divisions that have curtailed efforts in the past to pool knowledge and skills so as to solve complex scientific and societal problems. This fragmentation and isolation is not exclusive to the relationships between fields. Indeed, this is sometimes a problem even within traditional fields of science.

This state of affairs must change. The leadership role of the United States in science and technology has been put to new tests. Over the last five or so years, commencing roughly with the fall of the Berlin Wall, America has been adjusting to a new world position and defining a new national direction. The next several years will be a period of transition in which we will have the opportunity to build on our past successes but also to embrace new scientific challenges that will stretch us well beyond traditional disciplinary boundaries and narrowly focused pursuits.

The National Science Foundation, which was established to promote and enhance all fields of science and engineering, has, I believe, a unique role and opportunity here. As an institution, it is organized by grant-making divisions for various disciplines of science, engineering, and science education. In addition, it has established a cross-cutting structure to build links for interdisciplinary work.

This structure enables NSF to be more responsive to researchers with new ideas that do not fit the traditional mold and to show more explicitly how the activities the agency supports relate to important problems facing our society. The agency has also engendered some strong debate over so-called strategic research—or, as I prefer to call it, "research in strategic areas."

This use of the word *strategic* has confused and often inflamed scientists who feared that NSF was moving away from basic research. Not so! At NSF, strategic areas such as "global change and environmental research" or "high-performance computing and communication research" refer to research that is every bit as basic as the other research the agency supports that is related to larger national needs.

In addition to supporting innovative—often high-risk—approaches to research and education, however, NSF's further task, in these turbulent times of change, should be to pose the "unasked questions" to which there may not be ready answers. Such questions can serve to promote dialogue within the research and education community on issues that bear directly on its sustainability and prosperity as a community, as well as that of the nation.

Among the questions one might ask are: How can we overcome traditional cultural barriers in universities and funding agencies so as to enable better connections to form between disciplines? How do we evaluate interdisciplinary research ideas, outcomes, and the people who do the work? How do we insure maximum educational value for the students who are involved?

The answers to these questions are becoming clearer. We are seeing prominent successes in cases in which scientists from divergent disciplines are finding common ground and are discovering the importance of working collectively.

Good examples of this approach can be found at universities across the nation, where researchers are increasing their collaboration across the disciplines and with industry in a variety of ways. It is through such collaboration that researchers can overcome the fragmentation and separation that impede progress.

CONNECTIONS BETWEEN SCIENCE AND TECHNOLOGY

In some sense, the debate over research in strategic areas has its roots in an equally confusing and unsubstantiated debate over the distinction between basic and applied research. This debate has been going on for many years, at least since Vannevar Bush wrote his classic *Science: The Endless Frontier*.[4]

NSF is the primary overall supporter of taxpayer-funded basic research at academic institutions in nonbiomedical fields. This does not mean, however, that this research is lacking in a relationship to the nation's priorities and societal needs. The research may not be "applied," as the term is most often used, but it certainly is relevant.

Science is not simply about the future, it *is* the future. And, although we surely cannot forecast where and when discoveries will be made, research provides a process and a perspective that historically have produced new knowledge—knowledge that has again and again proven to be beneficial to the lives of people, when used to positive ends, and vital to sustaining the nation's stability and leadership in a turbulent world.

In the nineteenth century, T. H. Huxley rejected the proposition that no connections existed between so-called applied and pure science. Yet the debate continues. Huxley once said, "I often wish that this phrase 'applied science' had never been invented." To Huxley, this distinction suggested that there is scientific knowledge of direct practical use, which can be studied apart from another sort of scientific knowledge with no utility, known as pure science. According to Huxley, "There is no more complete fallacy than this."[5]

Donald Stokes, in his work entitled *Pasteur's Quadrant*, writes, "The annals of research so often record scientific advances simultaneously driven by the quest for both understanding and use that we are increasingly led to ask how it came to be so widely

---

[4] Vannevar Bush, *Science: The Endless Frontier* (Washington: U.S. Government Printing Office, 1945).

[5] T. H. Huxley, "Science and Culture," in *Great Essays in Science* (1880; reprint, Buffalo, N.Y.: Prometheus Books, 1994), 145.

believed that these goals are inevitably in tension and that the categories of basic and applied science are radically separated."[6] The title of Stokes's work comes from the example of the French scientist Louis Pasteur, who was influenced by public health and commercial goals throughout his stellar career in microbiology.

There are encyclopedias filled with examples to refute this separation that Stokes talks about. One might ask, then, why the debate in the scientific community about basic versus applied research is so fractious and why it sometimes includes contrived definitions, parameters, and even an elitist hierarchy of implied importance.

As French writer Eugene Ionesco once said, "It is not the answer that enlightens, but the question."[7] Asking why this friction and apparent mutual exclusivity have evolved would likely promote a healthy dialogue in the research community, not to determine a winner or a rigid answer but to explore, with openness and without prejudgment, an issue that ripples through our collective unconscious. Stokes's scholarship has provided guidance to help address this issue, but the members of the research community have to speak for and among themselves. Whether or not the dialogue leads to precise definitions of the meanings of basic and applied, it is important that the academic science community discuss its role in insuring that the knowledge and technologies that result from research do indeed reach those who would put them to good use.

NSF has long sought to increase its support for innovative partnerships that can overcome the artificial barriers between academic researchers and those in government laboratories and the private sector. Through its connections with the academic

---

[6] Donald Stokes, *Pasteur's Quadrant* (Washington, D.C.: Brookings Institute Press, 1995).

[7] Eugene Ionesco, *Decouvertes* (Geneva: Albert Skira, 1969).

community and industry, NSF has begun to create experimental strategies that seek to foster the connections between university and industry researchers. Through the Grant Opportunities for Academic Liaison with Industry (GOALI) program, for example, NSF is assisting scientists and engineers from universities and industry in working together in a variety of settings and encouraging collaboration at the conceptual stage of a research project.

More needs to be done in this area. To do that, agencies like NSF need the input of researchers in the university community. Two questions come to mind: In a time of decreasing federal support for scientific research, what new research activities is industry likely to support that are appropriate to the mission of the university? And how can we overcome the barriers to effective cooperation and collaboration between university researchers and scientists and engineers in industry?

The prospects in this area appear to be fairly bright, and they can be even brighter if researchers continue to work to effect important changes in the way they do business. We still have a way to go, but with the excellent collaborations between universities and industry, great strides are being made.

CONNECTIONS BETWEEN RESEARCH AND EDUCATION

Finally, a pivotal part of the much-needed dialogue between society and the academic community must reaffirm the value of the profoundly important connections between research and education—or, to put it another way, the integration of research and education. The beauty and dual utility of the "American" system of higher education, widely acclaimed as the best in the world, has been that the practice of research and teaching in the same place by the same people has capitalized on the natural and complementary connections between the process of education and that of discovery. Each is enhanced and enriched by the other.

From a certain perspective, both research and education are the same: they are both about learning.

There are, of course, good arguments for how research enhances undergraduate education at our universities and colleges. Classroom instruction at the undergraduate level is deeply enriched by a professor's personal excitement about his or her discoveries. Courses can be updated to reflect new discoveries when the faculty member stays on top of the developments. Undergraduate students—frequently through independent study courses and honors programs—work side by side in laboratories with faculty and graduate students, often designing their own research projects. Future elementary and high school teachers, who will be practicing inquiry-based instruction in their classrooms, can as undergraduates at least glimpse what discovery is all about by spending time with faculty and student researchers in their seminars and laboratories.

Many universities have taken positive steps toward ensuring that their research and education missions are kept closely linked. Most faculty, I believe, take for granted the importance of this link. For example, in a survey on the subject of teaching and research conducted by Oak Ridge Associated Universities of its sixty-five member colleges and universities, one professor said, "It would appear to me that if one . . . acknowledges that research is essentially teaching oneself, while instruction is teaching others, the interrelationship and symbiotic relationship between the two is inescapable." A senior vice president and provost said, "The undergraduate program is at the very heart of all that we do. . . . It is our responsibility to integrate cutting-edge research and technology into undergraduate education, to infuse the international dimension, and to develop the leadership skills of our students."[8]

[8] *Science or and Education* (Oak Ridge, Tenn.: Oak Ridge Associated Universities, 1995).

Nonetheless, all is not well in the public eye. Some feel too great an emphasis is placed on research to the detriment of undergraduate education. The important issue here is that the desired relationship between teaching and research cannot—at least should not —go undiscussed or unaddressed. This subject was the focus not only of a 60 *Minutes* piece but of several comments I made when I testified at the congressional hearing on NSF's budget reauthorization.

A senior, well-informed, science-supportive congressman expressed grave concern about what he perceived to be the separation of teaching and research on our campuses. He said a great many students at our universities never have the opportunity to take a class with an expert scientist because that person does not teach undergraduate classes.

It is clear that there will be increasing requests from Congress for accountability on the topic of the integration of research and education. Federal agencies such as NSF that fund research at universities will be held accountable for ensuring that this dual function of research and teaching is being carried out and that, indeed, research is not detrimental to undergraduate education.

NSF is committed to helping universities foster these important connections. It has created a few programs with the goal of integrating research and teaching and is increasing the amount of funds available for these initiatives. NSF's CAREER program is a notable example. CAREER awards provide a framework for junior-level university faculty to link their research projects with their teaching and mentoring responsibilities.

Another innovative NSF program is called Research Experiences for Undergraduates (REU). REU programs nationwide give undergraduates the chance to participate directly in research projects. On virtually every campus and at several National Laboratories I have visited, I have heard very positive comments about the program and the importance of keeping it strong.

NSF is not the only player, of course. CAREER and REU both complement and enhance innovations already under way designed to increase the natural link between teaching and research in universities.

Needless to say, agencies in Washington cannot provide unilateral solutions to this problem, nor should they; however, NSF and other federal research agencies need to examine their role in encouraging stronger links to be developed between teaching and research.

To address this issue, several questions need to be answered: Is the separation between research and education a perceived problem or a real problem? If real, why has the separation occurred in some departments, on some campuses? What are the external forces that contribute to such a separation? What are the internal forces within universities that can polarize these two ostensibly related functions?

Once again, it is not so much the answer that enlightens but the open articulation of the question. From this a dialogue can be initiated. Dialogues produce innovative changes and modifications from within. Dialogues also demonstrate to the public that its concerns are heard and that universities and colleges are trying to take action in response.

I am optimistic that we can have a sustainable, healthy science and technology enterprise well into the future. Although the much-revered "Golden Age of Science" is behind us and we are facing severe restrictions in the near-term federal budget, this need not mean that we cannot expect a new and sustainable Golden Age of Science a bit farther down the road. The university must be its core. This future Golden Age may not be the same as it was in the past, but it can be just as vital, just as exciting, and just as rewarding to the society that will be asked to support it.

Put another way, I cannot imagine the United States not being in a position of world leadership in the twenty-first century.

Nor can I see how the United States could be in that position without being a world leader in science and technology. It is not simply a matter of the large economic return on investment in research and development, or the knowledge and technologies needed—for national security, to protect the environment, to ensure our health and safety, to provide food and energy resources, to improve the education of our children and grandchildren, to improve communication and transportation. Important as these goals are, U.S. leadership in science and technology is necessary for another reason having to do with this nation's roots: there is a strong tradition in the United States of embarking on bold adventures of exploration, of taking risks, of making discoveries. That is what research in science and engineering is all about. This tradition has strong roots in America. We as a nation must think very carefully before giving it up.

A future Golden Age of Science will require increased investment, including federal investment. Once the public is convinced that spending is under control, people will be willing to talk about increasing the investment in the quality of life of their children and grandchildren. People care about education, and they care about science and technology. The issues are how much, what kind, and at what cost. But the costs of not investing have to be understood and weighed as well, and it is in identifying these costs that the science and technology community has to be involved.

This optimism given the current environment may sound a little foolish or even dreamlike. Another way to think of it is as a challenge, a challenge for all of us to come out from our laboratories and offices and sit down with the public and engage in a vigorous, positive discussion about the future of this nation.

If we in the academic and wider research community are going to answer this challenge, we must start to grapple with difficult questions about our own shops. That is necessary both to ensure the most effective use of the resources available and to gain the confidence of the business community and other leaders in our society whose support is necessary for our success. Indeed, we will need to convince them that our success is actually their success as well.

Reflecting back on history is sometimes helpful in gaining a useful perspective. About 500 million years ago, during the Ordovician period, there was great turmoil in some parts of the world as mountains were thrust upward as a result of collisions between tectonic plates. Yet it appears that the tectonic calamity led to a great blooming of life forms, both marine families and genera. Nature takes advantage of opportunity. We in the research community must do the same.

CHAPTER 7

Prospect for the Social Sciences in the Land Grant University

Urie Bronfenbrenner

ACCORDING TO THE Morrill Act, which became law on July 2, 1862, the original aim of a land grant university was to provide in each state "at least one college where the leading object [would] be, without excluding other scientific and classical studies, . . . such branches of learning as are related to agriculture and mechanical arts . . . in order to promote the liberal and practical education of the industrial classes in the several pursuits and professions of life."

The mission of the land grant university, both as stipulated in the Morrill Act and in its broader interpretation by the founders of land grant universities, has been expanded considerably over the years in content and scope. This extraordinary expansion occurred primarily in response to often dramatic changes, across successive decades, in the needs and problems arising in our society. As indicated in some of the data presented in this essay, nowadays such changes are occurring mainly in the social sphere and are likely to be even more dramatic and consequential in the coming century.

The progressive disarray of many of our most basic social institutions and in the society at large imperils the quality of life and the competence and character not only of the present generation but, perhaps even more, of generations to come. To anticipate the future fate of the social sciences in land grant universities, it is critical to understand the nature of the social changes taking place in American society and their most likely course in the future.

For several years now, about a dozen scholars at Cornell University, including graduate students and three extraordinarily able undergraduates, in fields ranging from economics to biopsychology, from infant development to aging, and from family processes to criminology, have been involved in a collaborative project, supported by a small grant from Cornell's College of Human Ecology, that seeks to investigate some of these pressing social issues.[1] This essay summarizes some of our findings and, in so doing, sets forth an agenda for social science research in land grant universities across the nation.

IS THE "AMERICAN DREAM" AT RISK?

Economic data indicate that Americans are finding it more difficult today than their parents did to realize the American dream of improving the conditions of life for themselves and their families and enabling their children to have even better lives. As shown in figure 7.1, over the twenty-six-year period from 1947 to

[1] The complete findings are in Urie Bronfenbrenner et al., eds., *The State of Americans: This Generation and the Next* (New York: Free Press, 1996). The author wishes to express special appreciation to Elliott Smith, an advanced doctoral student in the Department of Human Development and Family Studies at Cornell University, who not only has served very effectively as the administrative research coordinator for the project as a whole but has contributed significantly to the development of modes of analysis and forms of graphic presentation.

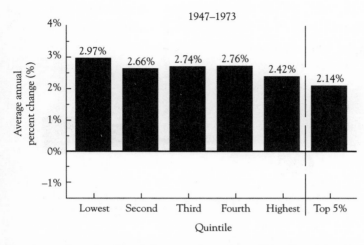

Figure 7.1 Growth of Family Income, Quintiles and Top 5%, 1947–73
Source: Bronfenbrenner et al., eds., *The State of Americans*, 61.

1973, economic conditions were improving for everybody, and especially for those who were least well off to start with.[2]

As illustrated in figure 7.2, the picture is quite different for the next nineteen years, from 1973 to 1992. A better life for one-self and one's children as one gets older is no longer possible for everyone. To repeat what is becoming a familiar refrain, the new reality is that the rich are getting richer, the poor are getting poorer, and, especially for the latter, working hard for the future may no longer pay off. In recent years, even the middle class has been experiencing less growth in its standard of living.

Over this same period, the federal deficit has been growing exponentially. Thus, American society no longer has anything like the resources required to finance a large-scale, emergency government program of economic recovery.

---

[2] The ideas and data presented in this section were developed by Peter McClelland, whose dual fields of expertise are economic history and mathematical models in economic analysis.

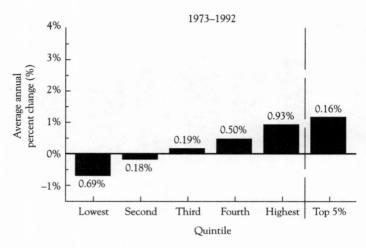

Figure 7.2 Growth of Family Income, Quintiles and Top 5%, 1973–92
Source: Bronfenbrenner et al., eds., *The State of Americans*, 61.

POVERTY AND THE NEXT GENERATION

As figure 7.3 shows, this new reality has been exacting heavy human costs.[3] Since the 1970s, the United States has been leading the developed world in having the highest percentage of children living in poverty. Next in line, albeit by several lengths, are other English-speaking countries; other West European nations trail well behind them.[4]

---

[3] The analyses on which the next two sections are based were developed and carried out by Helene Hembrooke, Pamela Morris, and Alanna Gelbwasser. The data presented in figure 7.3 appear in L. Rainwater, "Why the U.S. System Does Not Work Very Well," *Challenge*, Jan.–Feb. 1992, 30–35. These are the latest international data that are available. All pertain to the late 1980s or early 1990s. Since then, the poverty rate in the United States has been rising.

[4] Additional data on and discussion of this phenemenon appear in Urie Bronfenbrenner, "Child Care in the Anglo-Saxon Mode," in *Child Care in Context*, ed. M. E. Lamb, K. J. Sternberg, C. P. Hwang, and A. G. Broberg (Hillsdale, N.J.: Erlbaum), 281–91.

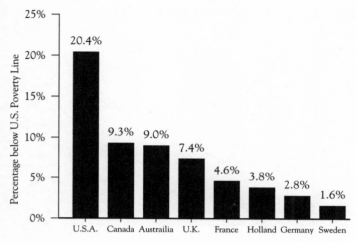

*Children are those under 18 years of age

Figure 7.3 Percentage of Children in Poverty in Developed Nations
Source: Bronfenbrenner et al., eds., *The State of Americans*, 148.

Has it always been this way, or is this a recent phenomenon? And what about the poverty rates for groups other than children?

Figure 7.4 addresses both questions. During the decade of high economic growth, from the early 1960s to the early 1970s, the percentage of children living in poverty dropped dramatically.[5] Then, as wages and other sources of income began to decline, poverty rates for families with young children began to rise and fall in response to short-term recessions and recoveries (indicated by the shaded bars), and, by the late 1970s, to begin their present upward course.

What fraction of America's children under six will be living in poverty at the turn of the century? The statistics for the elderly provide some clues. They have tumbled from 35 percent in 1959

[5] For the definition of poverty used in the graphs showing poverty rates in the United States, see U.S. Bureau of the Census, *Current Population Reports*, Series P60–188, *Income, Poverty and Valuation of Noncash Benefits: 1993* (Washington, D.C.: U.S. Government Printing Office), A1–A2.

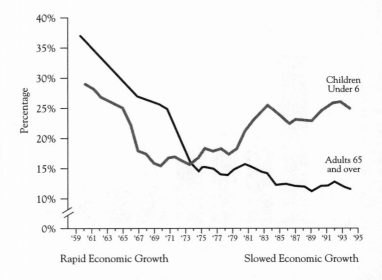

Figure 7.4 Percentage of Children under Six and Adults Sixty-five and over in Poverty in the United States
Source: Bronfenbrenner et al., eds., *The State of Americans*, 153.

and have kept falling, through economic rain and shine, to lows of less than 13 percent into the 1990s. The reason, of course, is social security income. As for the children of the poor, who do not have social security income, they and their parents live in two worlds divided by color. It is well known that poverty rates are higher for black families than for white. Figure 7.5 shows what is not so well known.

During the period of high economic growth in the 1960s and 1970s, there was a substantial drop in both black and white families in the percentages of young children living below the poverty line. Furthermore, whereas in 1959 two-thirds (68 percent) of all black children were living in poor families, a decade later that proportion had dropped to 40 percent, compared with a drop of 10 percent for whites. Thus, the gap between whites and blacks narrowed substantially from 45 percentage points in 1959

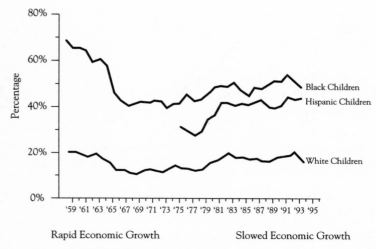

Figure 7.5 Poverty Rates among Young Children in the United States by Ethnic Groups
Source: Bronfenbrenner et al., eds., *The State of Americans*, 156.

to about 20 points in 1975. Moreover, although the poverty rates for both races rose during the period of declining economic growth that followed, black families have been able to hold their own, with the result that the racial gap has not increased.

There is also evidence that since the 1980s, families in poverty have increasingly been striving to make it on their own. For example, by 1994, in more than 60 percent of all such families with infants and/or preschoolers, at least one parent was working full time or part time. As of 1985, that figure was less than 40 percent.

At the same time, despite the fact that more parents in poor families have been working, their cash income from all sources has been declining. Thus, again by 1994, in 47 percent of these poor families in which at least one parent was working, the cash income from all sources was still 50 percent below the so-called poverty line—the income "cutoff" below which families become

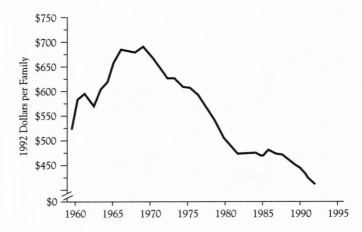

Figure 7.6 Average Monthly AFDC Payment per Family
Source: Bronfenbrenner et al., eds., *The State of Americans*, 160.

eligible to receive government assistance. Revised annually on the basis of the consumer price index, the poverty threshold takes into account such factors as family size, family structure, and the number of children in the family, although not their age. In 1994, to be 50 percent below the poverty line, the income of a two-parent family with two children under the age of eighteen could be no higher than $7,514, and for a single mother with only one child under the age of eighteen, it could be no higher than $5,964. Thus, in almost half of all poor families, this was all the money available to pay for food, housing, and other life necessities, even though one or both parents were working.

Why is the income in these families so low? Figure 7.6 gives us part of the answer.

About half of all poor families with children under six receive public assistance from the federal program Aid to Families with Dependent Children (AFDC). As figure 7.6 shows, while the average monthly payment rose during the decade of strong national economic growth in the 1960s, beginning in the 1970s, it began to

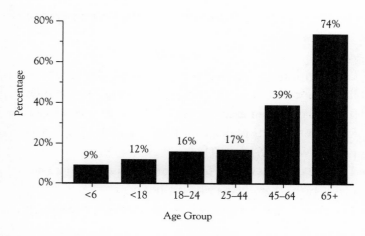

Figure 7.7 Government Assistance by Age Group in the United States
Source: Bronfenbrenner et al., eds., *The State of Americans,* 165.

fall at an equally rapid rate. By the 1990s, a family consisting of a single mother and two children had less than $10,000 a year to live on (including food stamps). To be sure, the progressive reductions were introduced to meet the needs of the growing numbers of young children in poverty. But, as revealed in figure 7.7, recipients in older age groups were accorded a progressively larger share of the available resources.

GROWING UP POOR: CONTEXTS AND CONSEQUENCES

What happens to children when they grow up in poverty "American style"? The most compelling evidence to answer this question comes from systematic investigations that have followed young children as they grew older and moved outside the home into other settings and relationships.

The results of these studies tell a consistent story that documents the high price our country pays for tolerating such high levels of poverty in families with young children. That price is paid in the competence and character of the next generation. To cite but a few examples:

- Children brought up in poverty are more than twice as likely as children of the nonpoor to drop out of high school. For those raised in poor families, the dropout rate for white students is almost as high as that for blacks (43 percent versus 46 percent).
- The rate of births among teenaged girls raised in poor families is twice that of girls who are not poor.
- The rate of crime is twice as high among youth brought up in poverty.
- Among poor families, the higher the level of the parents' education, the lower the risk that their child will drop out of school, their teenaged daughter will have a baby, or their son or daughter will engage in youth crime.

AMERICAN FAMILIES: TODAY AND TOMORROW

But it is not only the world of poor families that is changing. At all economic levels, more and more young children are growing up in homes in which there is only one parent (fig. 7.8). Compared with divorce rates for other developed nations, America is well in the lead (fig. 7.9).

In America today, single parenthood takes several different forms. Divorces and separations account for only some of the problem. As figure 7.10 reveals, the sharp rise in single parenthood that has been occurring in our country since the early 1970s is primarily the result of couples having children without getting married. It is mainly because of this phenomenon that more than a quarter of America's children are living in single-parent homes, and if current circumstances prevail, that figure is likely to continue to rise in the years ahead.

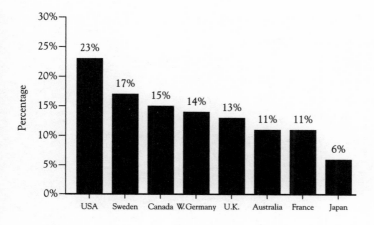

Figure 7.8 Incidence of Single-Parent Families in Developed Nations with Children under Eighteen
Source: Bronfenbrenner et al., eds., *The State of Americans*, 92.

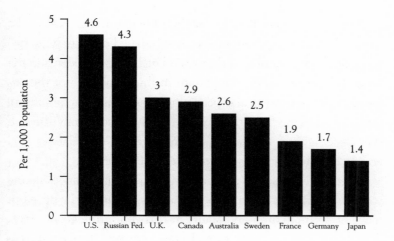

Figure 7.9 Incidence of Divorce in Developed Nations
Source: Bronfenbrenner et al., eds., *The State of Americans*, 93.

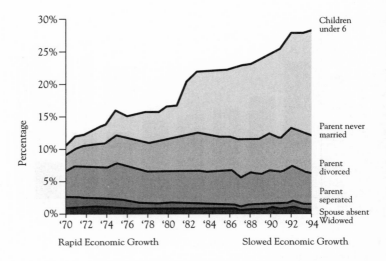

Figure 7.10 Percentage of Children under Six Being Raised by One Unmarried Parent
Source: Bronfenbrenner et al., eds., *The State of Americans,* 98.

Figure 7.11 identifies one of the principal influences on the level of sexual activity among our youth, based on a study by two researchers who sampled four thousand high school students in the state of Wisconsin.[6] Most important in this graph are not the differences between particular percentages but their general upward direction, moving from the two-parent biological family through the single mother, step family, and relatives, to nonrelatives, and ending back with a primary family tie—the father.

Also of relevance to a discussion of the social changes taking place in our society are how these changes will affect the development of both children and adults in this and future generations. The next figure begins to provide some answers. It also takes us

[6] T. Luster and S. A. Small, "Youth at Risk for Teenage Parenthood," paper presented at the Creating Caring Communities Conference, East Lansing, Mich., May 1990.

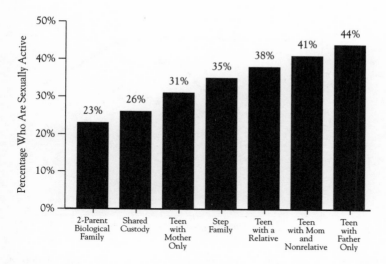

Figure 7.11 Sexual Activity among U.S. Teenagers, by Their Family Structure
Source: Bronfenbrenner et al., eds., *The State of Americans*, 117.

beyond the influence of the family to what is arguably the second most important institution in determining the competence and character of the next generation—our nation's schools.

Figure 7.12 shows that even when one compares the top 10 and 25 percent of twelfth graders in the United States with those from other developed countries, we still fall behind. In the words of Stephen J. Ceci, an outstanding cognitive psychologist and the expert in this area among the five Cornell faculty involved in the collaborative project: "This group [the top 10 percent and top 25 percent] is considered the raw material for the next generation's political leaders, science and engineering elite, and business managers, [yet] American students tend to be nearer the achievement levels of Italy and Thailand in such comparisons than to Japan, Sweden, and England."[7]

---

[7] Stephen J. Ceci, "American Education: Looking Inward and Outward," in *The State of Americans*, ed. Urie Bronfenbrenner et al., 204.

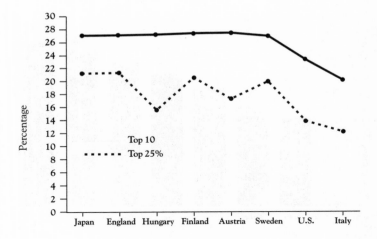

Figure 7.12 International Comparison of Raw Scores of Twelfth Graders on Math and Science Achievement Tests, 1990
Source: Bronfenbrenner et al., eds., *The State of Americans*, 199.

Ceci is quick to point out, however, that there is some good news along with the bad. In particular, he calls attention to the fact that black children, the group long obtaining the lowest achievement test scores, have shown notable gains over the past twenty years. On the basis of his analysis of the available data, Ceci credits such improvement to the substantial financial and political investment that took place: "Educational spending is up over 250 percent in real dollars during this same period, with increases in spending disproportionally targeted to programs serving minority youngsters (e.g., Title 1, Head Start, lunch programs)."[8] He also emphasizes the indirect effect of gains in the educational attainment of parents on their children's development.

Clearly, both families and schools play a major role in influencing outcomes in a domain of special significance for the future

[8] Ibid., 194.

of any society—namely, in shaping the attitudes, values, and behaviors of those who will take on the roles and responsibilities of adults in the society.[9] Our analyses in this area are based on results of two major national surveys that have been carried out on an annual basis for many years. The first, entitled "Monitoring the Future," documents responses from the nation's high school seniors from 1977 to 1994. The second, "The American Freshman," covers an even longer time span beginning ten years earlier, in 1967.

Based on our evaluations so far, the overall trend is unmistakable—and the same for both age groups. There is growing cynicism about self and society. It is manifested in such diverse domains as loss of faith in the future, in academic integrity, in trust in human relationships, in government, and in participation in the political process. Also salient is a reduced readiness to take learning seriously, as well as a greater emphasis on materialism and on the importance of "making money" as a lifetime goal. Finally, most disturbing of all, there is a trend toward an increased tolerance of violence.

The most pronounced trend (fig. 7.13) is that since 1980 young people have contributed significantly to the doubling of the national homicide rate, from 7.6 percent in 1984 to 16.4 percent in 1993, and represent a substantial fraction of the tremendous increase since 1970 in the number of prison inmates held in local, state, and federal penal institutions (fig. 7.14). We have not yet been able to find any firm figures on the economic costs of maintaining these facilities and building more, let alone the physical and psychological costs to the victims of violence, the fear of danger experienced by increasing segments of the population as they engage in everyday social and economic activities, and the general emotional state that this fear engenders not only among adults but among children.

[9] Our expert in this area is Elaine Wethington, a medical sociologist.

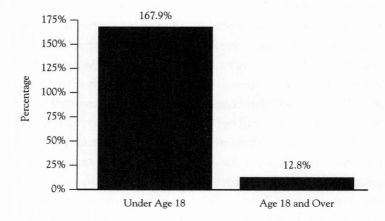

Figure 7.13 Percentage Increase in the Number of Arrests for Homocide in the United States, 1984–93
Source: Bronfenbrenner et al., eds., *The State of Americans*, 33.

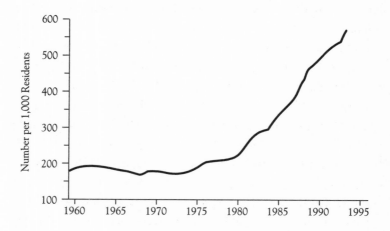

Figure 7.14 Number of Inmates in Local Jails, State Prisons, and Federal Prisons
Source: Bronfenbrenner et al., eds., *The State of Americans*, 36.

Yet another major social change creates new dilemmas but may also offer some relief with respect to the problems documented thus far (fig. 7.15): the age structure of the American population is changing, a trend that is certain to become even more pronounced in the decades ahead. Cornell professor Phyllis Moen, whose research is focused in this sphere and who alerted us to its importance, points out that in effect we are dealing with two different groups living in two different ecologies. There are what might be called the "aging elderly"—those Americans who are predominantly eighty-five and over—and the "younger elderly"—who constitute the majority of those under seventy-five. Most of the former will require large outlays for extended periods of time to meet the cost of their highly expensive medical services, as well as facilities for residential care. By contrast, many, if not the majority, of the younger elderly are still highly competent, well educated, and have much leisure time at their disposal. Many use this time for volunteer activities and for extending their education. Thus, they represent a growing potential resource for carrying out socially and

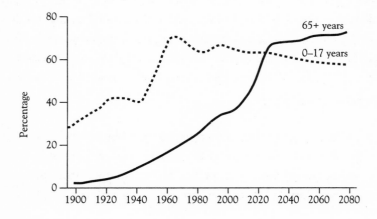

Figure 7.15 Trends in the Age Structure of the U.S. Population, 1940–2080
Source: Bronfenbrenner et al., eds., *The State of Americans,* 213.

economically productive activity directed at counteracting the disruptive social and economic trends occurring in the society.[10]

At the same time, demographic studies indicate that as the numbers of elderly in the population are increasing, the proportions of children, youth, and young adults are declining at a comparable or even greater rate. This means that the prevalence of the problems related to competence and character currently associated with these younger cohorts will decrease. Nevertheless, to the extent that these problems are the product of prevailing social conditions and existing policies and practices, the severity of these deficiencies and disruptive behaviors is likely not only to continue but to increase in degree. They are also likely to be manifested in more severe forms among the adults of tomorrow, who are the youth of today.

RELATIONSHIP BETWEEN SOCIAL CHANGES AND MISSION OF LAND GRANT UNIVERSITIES

As I stated at the beginning of this essay, the mission of the land grant university is much broader today both in scope and substance than it was in its early years. As defined by a committee chaired by Norman R. Scott, vice president for research and advanced studies, and also a professor of agriculture and biological engineering, the expanded mission of Cornell University, for example, encompasses

a broad range of outreach programs, including technology transfer, professional and executive education, extension, research consortia and public policy analysis [through which] Cornell University connects daily with the people

[10] See Phyllis Moen, "Change Age Trends: The Pyramid Upside Down?" in *The State of Americans*, ed. Urie Bronfenbrenner et al., 212–66.

of the state, nation, and world. The knowledge generated by a great research university is interpreted by faculty and educators in thousands of practical ways. Cornell's outreach efforts should build on and strengthen the research of the University to address key social, economic, health, environmental, and cultural issues. Outreach is important to every one of Cornell's schools and colleges. It is both a tradition and a new opportunity for the twenty-first century, to contribute to society and justify society's continued support of Cornell.[11]

What, then, is the prospect for the social sciences in the context of this broadened commitment to outreach? In answering that question, I shall begin with a caveat to which some social scientists might take strong exception. In the physical and biological sciences, outreach often means not only providing new knowledge but also providing effective solutions to major problems confronting the society; for example, more powerful and efficient fuels or successful methods of disease prevention. In the social sciences, outreach often means providing new knowledge, to be sure, but at best very few solutions are offered that have survived extensive, rigorous field trials.

The reason for this deficiency does not imply any failure to recognize the importance of the social sciences but rather that social scientists do not possess the degree of precision in theory and corresponding empirical work that points clearly and unambiguously to strategies of implementation that have a high probability of success as, for example, in the case of designing vehicles for exploring outer space.

11 Norman R. Scott and Lucinda Noble, "Cornell's Outreach Obligation," paper presented at Academic Leadership Series on Outreach, Cornell University, Ithaca, N.Y., May 1995.

Yet the justification for outreach in the social sciences is equally urgent, and equally practicable; namely, to investigate, identify, and communicate the nature and scope of the problems that our society is facing. Not only is such knowledge necessary to find effective solutions but, in the absence of such knowledge, applying strategies without first subjecting them to rigorous scientific analysis and smaller-scale pretesting of their effects carries the risk both of wasting much-needed resources and of doing even greater damage to human beings, particularly if the proposed solutions are simplistic in nature.

One other element is essential if social scientists are to meet their responsibilities not only to land grant universities but to science and society as a whole. This element was prominent, if not preeminent, in the original statement in the Morrill Act of 1862 that described the mission of the land grant university; namely, "to promote liberal and practical education"—in short, teaching the younger generation. If the founders of land grant universities were correct, as I believe they were, in expanding the land grant mission in response to the critical new problems confronting the society at large, then, in light of the evidence and argument presented here, the social sciences today face a special challenge and responsibility—that is, to inform the future leaders of our society about the nature, extent, and consequences of the social problems confronting the nation and to engage them in a common effort to address these problems in a responsible and disciplined way, not only in the classroom but in real-life settings outside the university.

Within this framework, it becomes the role of social scientists in land grant universities to take the lead in defining and pursuing this joint effort in research, teaching, and outreach. The extent to which they meet this threefold challenge may well determine the answer to the question of whether the American university is a national treasure or an endangered species.

The American University: National Treasure or Endangered Species?

Frank H. T. Rhodes

I WELCOME THE OPPORTUNITY to express my grati-
tude to those who planned and participated in the symposium
which resulted in this volume. Some time ago, Peter Stein, dean
of the Cornell faculty, told me that the Faculty Council of
Representatives wished to hold a symposium to mark my retirement, and he invited me to suggest a topic for the symposium.
This, of course, I was happy to do and that is how the title—
"The American University: National Treasure or Endangered
Species?"—came into existence. I chose the title largely because
in the current debate most observers would regard those two
characterizations of the university as polar positions.

Happy as I was to be allowed to suggest the topic for this symposium, I was no less happy to be allowed to invite the participants.
I chose, in fact, the most knowledgeable people I could think of in
each of the various areas and, to my delight, each of them agreed
to come. I should add, by way of full disclosure, that the speakers
were individuals who have been not only colleagues over many
years—in some cases more than twenty years—but also people

whom I am privileged to count as friends, as were those who served as chairs and panelists during this symposium.

So let me express my collective thanks to Brett de Bary, Ron Ehrenberg, Peter Stein, Yervant Terzian, and Jerry Ziegler, who formed the planning committee for this symposium, and also to Bill Bowen, Urie Bronfenbrenner, Marye Anne Fox, Hanna Gray, Neal Lane, Harold Shapiro, and Chuck Vest, who were our speakers.

I also want to thank those many faculty colleagues who were present for a day and a half to share in what was a remarkable gathering. It has been said that old presidents never die, they simply lose their faculties. I was therefore immensely reassured to see that the large number of faculty who were present at the beginning of this symposium were also present at the conclusion of the symposium. To all those who participated, I extend my sincere appreciation.

At the end of the symposium, my colleagues generously gave me the opportunity to respond to the splendid talks and discussions which had characterized the proceedings. It is the substance of those comments that I reproduce here.

First, is the American university a national treasure? I would argue that it is. The university as we know it in this country is one of the great creations of the human spirit, created here over a period of 350 years, but acknowledging its roots in Europe nine centuries ago. The distinctive American university is a remarkable institution: part private, part public, part planned, part opportunistically emergent, proudly independent, self-confident, inventive, creative, and competitive. It is, perhaps, the one institution in our nation that is by common consent agreed to be the best of its kind in the world. Any ranking of the world's top twenty universities would, I think, identify a dozen or so of them as being in this country.

In what ways have the universities proved to be a national trea-sure? They have, of course, educated generations of students, many of whom have gone on to positions of large responsibility and careers of great distinction in every field of endeavor. That univer-sities have won the support and affection of their students is demonstrated by contributions and gifts from grateful alumni, which in several recent fund-raising campaigns have exceeded $1 billion. Yet they have achieved this success not by restricting access to the wealthy and the powerful but by enlarging it. They have been leaders in providing social mobility and upward advancement for the underrepresented, and their commitment to equal opportunity challenges the rest of society to match their progress.

Their scholarship and research have also produced enormous social benefits, ranging from health care to new technology to sci-entific discovery. Confirmation is to be found in so many things we now take for granted which had their origin in the laboratories and libraries of our universities. Whole new industries, such as biotech-nology and computing, have arisen as a result of discoveries made in the universities, while major advancements in everything from surgical techniques to agricultural productivity have resulted from their professional service and leadership. It is no accident that the great majority of Nobel laureates of the last half-century are either graduates of, or teachers in, major American research universities.

And in spite of current economic pressures, universities are besieged by applicants for admission, both from our own country and from overseas. Universities in the United States are now *the* institutions of choice for the world's graduate students. More than 50 percent of the doctoral degrees in some fields of science and engineering are now awarded to students from other countries.

In addition to their successful educational and research pro-grams, the universities have pioneered the concept of community service, not only through the land grant tradition of public universities—now well over a century old and growing ever stronger—but also through outreach and service provided by the independent universities. From the Bronx to Botswana, thousands of local communities can testify to the effectiveness of programs, support, and service provided by teams of university researchers.

By any realistic assessment there is much to celebrate in the achievement of our universities. One would not, of course, gather that from the criticisms to which universities have recently been exposed. These criticisms involve allegations of the unreasonably high tuition, the neglect of undergraduate teaching in favor of inconsequential research, garbled educational purposes, fragmented fields of study, and trivialized scholarship. Nor has the noneducational work of the universities escaped harsh criticism. It is claimed by some that conflicts of interest exist in some research, that falsification of experimental results in science and improper accounting techniques have tarnished the university's role as impartial critic and inquirer, while the preaching of politics and the imposition of political correctness have chilled the climate of campus life. Universities, our critics assert, are self-indulgent, arrogant, and resistant to change, more interested in promoting the interests of their faculty than in providing some vision, or competing visions, of what an educated person should be.

It would be difficult to argue that none of these sharp accusations has any merit, but those who know the universities well will recognize that, though inevitably there are horror stories here and there, these complaints do not characterize the majority of institutions.

But let me ask whether, although they are national treasures, it might also be that our universities are endangered species. As a student of both universities and species, it seems to me that question calls for some reflection. So let me, for a moment, resume my role as professor of geology. After all, every species now endangered was once successful, having developed in an environment to which it became adapted. Extinction—one possible fate for an endangered species—generally follows either some marked change in the environment, sometimes catastrophic—as in the late Cretaceous event that did in the dinosaurs—or sometimes more gradual, as in the mid- and late Tertiary changes that so influenced mammalian evolution. In other cases, the environment to which the species had become adapted became steadily more restricted, with the species becoming narrowly, although sometimes exquisitely, specialized. And in still other cases, it seems that internal weaknesses or disease may have been contributing factors in the extinction of endangered species.

So, over the course of geologic time, almost all species become extinct; only in a few cases do organisms survive for very long, and those that do are often greatly reduced in numbers and in range. The coelacanth, living in deep waters off Madagascar, is such an example.

And what of universities? I suggest that the external environment of the university has changed. It has changed relatively rapidly and markedly in a way that suggests we are facing not a temporal fluctuation but a fundamental structural change to which we must adapt or face decline. Other societal priorities, for example, now crowd upon the need for public and private funding, so that California is reported to spend more on its prisons than it does on education. These competing societal needs mean, I believe, that funding constraints will not only be with us for some appreciable time but that they may well grow even more severe. These constraints, incidentally, exist not only in the United States but in most other industrial nations as well.

Nor is this all, for it is argued that the number and scope of degrees awarded by our universities now bear little relation to national needs. Stories of unemployed Ph.D.s in physics and overproduction of medical specialists are sadly more than anecdote and folklore. And the pattern of research support, on which universities have come to depend, is now threatened, if not by reduction, then by *stasis*, which is likely to diminish the support of existing studies and inhibit the development and growth of new areas of inquiry.

Universities encounter these constraints at the very time that intellectual opportunities and societal needs become ever greater, both from the advance in knowledge itself and from the social demands which are placed on them. Rarely have public expectations and societal needs been so high, and the level of public support and understanding of universities so low. This paradox is of more than casual interest, and it suggests that universities must help themselves if they are to be effective. Of course they will survive. Of that I have no doubt. Clark Kerr has reminded us that about eighty-five institutions in the Western world established by 1522 still exist in recognizable forms, with similar functions and with unbroken histories. These include the Catholic Church, the parliaments of the Isle of Man, of Iceland, and of Great Britain, several Swiss cantons, and seventy universities.

"Kings that rule, feudal lords with vassals, and guilds with monopolies are all gone. These seventy universities, however, are still in the same locations with some of the same buildings, with professors and students doing much the same thing, and with governments carried out in much the same ways," Clark Kerr reflects.

But survival is not enough. Survival should not be our ultimate goal. Effectiveness, vigor, and creativity are supremely important characteristics. Universities must be nimble, flexible, and responsive to the changing needs of society and the changing opportunities for understanding if they are to serve our generation well.

Having said that, let me add that, while I think there is little prospect of extinction, the greatest perils lie not from dangers without, but from weaknesses within universities. If we are candid, we know that universities are weakened every time their practices betray their rhetoric. They are weakened every time the experience of undergraduates belies the glowing language of their college catalogs. They are weakened every time narrow personal interests override the needs for collegiality and the wider interests of the academic community. They are weakened when they ignore practices that diminish their effectiveness and tolerate organizations that provide disincentives for both individual development and collegiality. They are weakened when narrow interests subvert the larger interests of the community, and they are weakened when administrative leadership allows the second best to flourish at the expense of the best. Universities are places of extraordinary privilege and freedom, created by a tolerant public and supported by private and public beneficence. But with that privilege and freedom there goes great responsibility, and it is that, I sometimes fear, which is in short supply. There are, it seems to me, half a dozen basic requirements that are necessary if universities are to avoid internal degeneration and remain flexible and responsive to changing societal needs, while still retaining distinction in teaching, research and scholarship:

- They require bold, decisive, and visionary leadership from those in positions of authority, especially presidents, provosts, and deans.
- They require effective and imaginative management of resources, not only at the institutional level but especially at the departmental level, and especially a greater determination than they have yet shown to constrain and reduce burgeoning costs.
- They require a new commitment to clients, among whom I include students—to whom they have their first and largest obligation, both as the chief providers of revenue and as those for whose benefit they were created—as well as alumni and society at large.
- They require a more general willingness to come to terms

with new expectations, unacknowledged issues—such as the loss of mandatory retirement—and constrained levels of funding in research, which will, I believe, constrain the areas of scholarship represented on many campuses and perhaps change the traditional balance between teaching and research.

• They require the restoration of community, which will come about only when universities create rewards and incentives for engagement and cooperation across the campus.

• And, finally, they require new patterns of governance, especially in the public universities, which are now in serious disrepair.

I shall not presume to elaborate on what each of these will require on particular campuses, but I do realize that confronting these issues will involve not only a measure of inconvenience, and perhaps consternation, but also lively debate and both personal and institutional reorientation. That seems to be an inevitable, but not necessarily undesirable, outcome. It is easy to grow complacent, denying the reality of the need for change, insulated as universities generally are from many of the external pressures.

If you are not persuaded that universities must confront these new realities, let me suggest that you read half a dozen successive copies of the *Chronicle of Higher Education* and then consider whether or not conscious adaptation will not be required for the survival of the institutional species that we represent. And if you argue that institutions like ours are not, and indeed should not be, subject to the pressures of the marketplace, I can only remind you of the fate that has befallen our medical centers and hospitals in the last decade. Ten years ago, health care was regarded as sacrosanct, and hospitals were inviolable. Today, all that has changed, and the change continues apace. If universities do not seize the opportunity to adapt themselves to changed circumstances, others will impose adaptation upon them.

But there is another reason for universities to embrace change, more compelling than that of mere survival. I believe the health and quality of scholarship will benefit from thoughtful change and that the requirements I have outlined will, in fact, improve the quality of scholarship.

Most of us, I suppose, entered the academic profession because we believed that teaching is a moral vocation, that scholarship is a public trust, and that service is a societal obligation. I believe that, for most of us, those basic affirmations have not changed, even though the environment in which we pursue our calling has changed.

But, in spite of the external threats, I remain an optimist. And I am optimistic not because I minimize the severity of the threats that face universities, but because I have come to know the faculty at Cornell well over the past eighteen years. They, my colleagues and my friends, embody, I believe, the qualities that we prize in the world of the university. Capable, knowledgeable, wise, responsible, committed, and friendly, not only to disputation, but also to one another. I believe we have here a community of compelling value and significance, reflecting as it does the conviction that scholarship is a public trust and not a private indulgence.

Our high calling was never better described than by Alfred North Whitehead when he declared, "The task of the university is the creation of the future so far as rational discourse and civilized means of appreciation can affect the issue."

Neal Lane, in his speech, quoted one line from John Masefield. That line was taken from a speech Masefield—then the poet laureate of England—gave in 1946 at the installation of a new vice chancellor at a red brick university, the University of Sheffield. 1946 was not a particularly pleasant time in England. It had shared with its allies in winning a war, but it was stumbling incoherently into the new peace, almost bankrupt, food, fuel, and clothing still rationed, and with many of its cities and industries in ruins. Amidst this gloom, Masefield offered a light and hope: "There are few earthly things more splendid than a university," he said. "Wherever it exists, it stands and shines. It stands and shines so that the free minds of men [and women], urged on to full and fair inquiry, may still bring wisdom to bear in human affairs."

I believe our universities and their faculties, personified by the speakers, the discussants, and my Cornell colleagues for the past eighteen terrific years, embody that lofty role, reflect that splendid calling, and embrace that moral vocation. For the support and inspiration they have provided over these long years, no less than for the wisdom of these essays, I offer my heartfelt thanks.

CONTRIBUTORS

WILLIAM G. BOWEN is the president of The Andrew W. Mellon Foundation.

URIE BRONFENBRENNER is a professor in the Department of Human Development and Family Studies at Cornell University.

RONALD G. EHRENBERG is the vice president for academic programs, planning, and budgeting at Cornell University.

MARYE ANNE FOX is the vice president for research at the University of Texas, Austin.

HANNA H. GRAY is president emeritus and professor of history at the University of Chicago.

NEAL LANE is the director of the National Science Foundation.

FRANK H. T. RHODES is president emeritus of Cornell University.

HAROLD T. SHAPIRO is the president of Princeton University.

PETER C. STEIN is professor of physics and the dean of the university faculty at Cornell University.

CHARLES M. VEST is the president of the Massachusetts Institute of Technology.